**Rethinking Military Politics**

ALFRED STEPAN

# Rethinking Military Politics

Brazil and the Southern Cone

PRINCETON UNIVERSITY PRESS

Published by Princeton University Press, 41 William Street,
Princeton, New Jersey 08540
In the United Kingdom: Princeton University Press,
Chichester, West Sussex

Library of Congress Cataloging in Publication Data will be
found on the last printed page of this book

ISBN  0-691-07750-9 (cloth)
          0-691-02274-7 (pbk.)

Publication of this book has been aided by the Whitney Darrow
Fund of Princeton University Press

Princeton University Press books are printed on acid-free paper
and meet the guidelines for permanence and durability of the
Committee on Production Guidelines for Book Longevity of the
Council on Library Resources

Printed in the United States of America

10   9   8   7   6   5   4

TO M.L.T.Q.S.

# CONTENTS

# LISTS OF TABLES AND FIGURES

TABLES

FIGURES

# PREFACE

FOR MAX WEBER, "the monopoly of the legitimate use of physical force" is part of the very definition of the modern state.[1] For polities that aspire to be democracies, a complex range of norms, institutions, and practices must be constructed socially, constantly reconstructed, and continually brought to bear so that a democratic polity in fact shapes, monitors, and controls the means of force that are an intrinsic part both of its "stateness" and its democracy.

In the United States, for example, the fact that a substantial percentage of our GNP (6.6 percent in 1983) is spent on defense-related items means that great material interests are at stake for the polity.[2] As the 1987 Iran-Contra scandal illustrates, when arguments based on *raison d'état* are linked to the inevitable tendency of security organizations to attempt to act with secrecy and autonomy, democratic control of policy is challenged severely. Nuclear weapons make the democratic control of force even more important and yet more difficult. In the internal politics of nuclear-weapons control and management, two structural pressures are now routinely and legally at play. The claims of state-military secrecy are extremely high, as are the claims of state-military expertise. Both of these tend to reduce the scope of significant decisions about force that are in fact regulated by democratic procedures.[3] It is almost axiomatic, therefore, that increased democratic control of the means of force in the United States requires conscious strategies of self-empowerment by democratic actors in society at large

[1] Max Weber, "Politics as a Vocation," 78. Weber's full statement is: "[A] state is a human community that (successfully) claims the *monopoly of the legitimate use of physical force* within a given territory." (Emphasis in original.)

[2] In 1983 this amounted to 220 billion dollars. See United States Arms Control and Disarmament Agency, *World Military Expenditures and Arms Transfers, 1985* (August 1985), 85. For the definition of what constitutes "military expenditures," see 139–141.

[3] For an illuminating discussion of this problem, see Robert Dahl, *Controlling Nuclear Weapons: Democracy Versus Guardianship*, esp. Chapter 1.

and specifically in our political organizations. The claims of state-military expertise can be met only by the conscious effort to develop capacities within civil and political society to speak with knowledge and authority on complex matters of geopolitics, arms, security, and peace. Claims of secrecy can be countered only by rigorous efforts at oversight and accountability, and by the attempt to generate and share information relevant to war and peace.[4]

The problems of force and violence in a long-established democracy are difficult; even more are they difficult in "newly democratizing" ones. The overthrow of tyrannies in the Philippines and Haiti, the movement toward democratic consolidation in Spain, Portugal, and Greece, the termination of bureaucratic-authoritarian regimes in Brazil, Argentina, and Uruguay, and the efforts to end dictatorships in Chile and South Korea have revivified debates about the fundamental issues involved in the forging of new democracies. Political parties, foundations, public monies, and academic inquiry have generated numerous collective projects on the subject. It would seem self-evident that the renewed public attention to democracy would entail a serious examination of the problem of how to manage the military democratically. Such an examination would seem to be fundamental to our analysis of the weakening of authoritarian regimes, of democratic transition, and democratic consolidation for three reasons. First, the military either heads or provides the core of the coercive state apparatus of most authoritarian regimes. Second, most of the would-be "successor" democratic regimes are immediately faced with major problems as to how to control and redirect the military and intelligence systems they inherit. Third, the military often continues to represent a critical component in politics by offering, implicitly or otherwise, a threatening alternative to democracy. For all of these reasons a democratic *strategy* toward the military (in Spanish, a

---

[4] For excellent examples of how both the claim of expertise and the claim of secrecy can be effectively contested in an area such as the Comprehensive Test Ban Treaty debates, see Lynn R. Sykes and Jack F. Evernden, "The Verification of a Comprehensive Nuclear Test Ban," and Paul G. Richards and Allan Lindle, "Toward a New Test Ban Regime."

"*política militar*") would appear to be a necessary condition of redemocratization movements.

Unfortunately, for a variety of reasons discussed in this book, the military has probably been the least studied of the factors involved in new democratic movements. For instance, in Brazil, in the first decade of the political "opening" of the authoritarian system, there was an outpouring of critical publications on authoritarianism in general, and on torture in particular. Yet virtually no systematic publications in any language appeared on the role of the military in the process of liberalization. In many of the newly democratizing polities, the absence of a tradition of autonomous civilian thought about military affairs is now emerging as a critical problem. For reasons of policy and theory, therefore, there is a pressing need to "rethink" the problem of the military in politics, normatively, politically, and methodologically.

I am primarily concerned with the military dimension of authoritarian regimes, the role of the military in the process of transition from authoritarianism to democracy, the continued part the military play in constraining the consolidation of many newly democratic regimes, and strategies of democratic empowerment vis-à-vis the military. My main focus is on Brazil, about which I have been writing since 1964, the year the first military regime of the twentieth century came to power in that country.[5] This military regime proved to be a new kind of regime, some of whose characteristics were found later in other nations of the southern cone of South America in the 1970s.[6] In the more recent "transition" away from authoritarianism, the military in these countries left legacies in civil-military relations that are powerful obstacles,

[5] I was in Brazil in 1964 as a special foreign correspondent for *The Economist* and wrote about the military coup. I later wrote *The Military in Politics: Changing Patterns in Brazil*.

[6] In a seminal discussion, Guillermo O'Donnell described these regime characteristics and categorized them under the label, "bureaucratic-authoritarianism." See his *Modernization and Bureaucratic-Authoritarianism: Studies in South American Politics*. For an important review of the literature and arguments associated with this term, see David Collier, ed., *The New Authoritarianism in Latin America*.

both ideologically and practically, to the difficult tasks of extending and consolidating democratic rule. The countries of the southern cone—Argentina, Chile, and Uruguay—are incorporated in my analysis, together with Spain. The intent is to be broadly comparative throughout the book.

This book opens in Chapter 1 with a discussion of several puzzling questions in the sociology of knowledge. Why have the military been so neglected in contemporary research and how has this neglect distorted our analyses of authoritarian regimes and democratizing movements? I am particularly interested in identifying those features of military politics that have sufficient regularity, specificity, and significance to require that we accord the military some independent theoretical status as an actor, instead of merely subsuming them in larger categories such as the "state," or even in regime categories such as "bureaucratic-authoritarianism."

The military regimes in Brazil, Argentina, Chile, and Uruguay were all associated with an expansion of military-mission definition, organizational reach, and comparative power. In Chapter 2, I explore the concrete institutional forms this expansion took, especially the new intelligence services. Specifically, I evaluate what organizational functions, capacities, and interests came to be associated with the military-intelligence operations in these countries and the impact they had on other components of the state as well as on civil and political society.

In Chapter 3, I analyze the first steps in the transition in Brazil from authoritarian to democratic rule. The Brazilian transition is one of the longest in the history of such transitions and in some important respects is not yet complete. I seek to demonstrate that the most critical motivation for the initial opening of the authoritarian regime had its origins in contradictions within the state generated by the development of the new, relatively autonomous military intelligence and repressive systems. These contradictions led one component of the military itself to seek allies in civil society. A complex dialectical process of "regime concession and societal conquest" ensued.

In Chapter 4, I turn to an examination of formal doctrine within the military, in order to discover what it can reveal about the military outlook on the process of democratic transition. I explore what the original *distensão* (decompression), and the broader opening that came to be called *abertura*, changed—and did not change. The most widely accepted source for the formulation and dissemination of national military doctrine in Brazil is the Superior War College (ESG), and it is the college's publications during the abertura that I evaluate. I supplement this analysis with interviews with military officers. My "discourse analysis" reveals how the military made constant modifications to these doctrines during the abertura while managing nevertheless to structure tightly the terms of the debate about what were acceptable parameters of conflict in the polity. I conclude that by the time of the election in 1982, changes in formal doctrine and informal attitudes in the military were supportive of *liberalization*; however, the overwhelming weight of doctrine, law, and attitude was well short of accepting *democratization*.[7]

In Chapter 5, the subject discussed is regime termination. I review the changes in the power relationships within the authoritarian state apparatus, civil society, and political society between 1970 and 1982. I argue that although the authoritarian regime in 1982 was much weaker in relational terms than it had been in 1970, it was not in disarray. In my judgment, the existing balance of power in 1982 was consistent with the military's expressed desire to postpone the possibility of democratic alternation in power, and therefore the opposition's electoral victory (core characteristics of democracy) until 1991. Between 1982 and 1984, however, the fundamental power relationship that changed was the growing autonomy of political society (both within the pro- and the antiregime components). Changes in this sphere further weakened the military's resolve to maintain the regime, and brought the opposition in civil and political society closer together. In this new power setting, it was the intense and creative transactions of polit-

---

[7] The distinction between "liberalization" and "democratization" is elaborated upon in Chapter 1, as is my usage of "civil society," "political society," and the "state."

ical society that prepared the way for the swearing in of a civilian opposition leader, Tancredo Neves, as president on March 15, 1985. Though Tancredo Neves's death through illness precluded his presidency, the period represented the termination of the military regime.

The last three chapters of the book turn to problems the military create for the consolidation of new democracies. Even when the original authoritarian "project" is no longer present, and the associated alliance structure is substantially changed, the military are normally quite present within the polity in one form or another. Failure to assess the specificity of their presence, the legacies the specific path taken to democracy leaves, and the continued problems of how, in practice, to monitor and control the means of force in society is costly to political actors and theoreticians alike.

Paying particular attention to patterns of civil-military relations in the three former bureaucratic-authoritarian regimes of Brazil, Argentina, and Uruguay, and because of the telling contrasts that emerge, to Spain, I assess the degree of articulated military opposition to the new democratic leaders (Chapter 6), the formal and informal prerogatives the military often still retain in new democracies and their consequences for the democratic management of the military (Chapter 7), and the potential strategies of empowerment vis-à-vis the military that could be developed within civil society, political society, and the state (Chapter 8).

The themes in these three chapters concern the military dimensions to the obstacles to democratic consolidation. The nature of the specific transition from military to democratic rule has a major impact on the comparative weight and power of the military within successor regimes. In Brazil, for example, the military relinquished their control of the presidency in 1985 only after intense informal negotiations that left many military prerogatives unchallenged. Indeed, in the twelve years between 1973 and 1985, the military were able to reconstitute their internal hierarchy and create new capacities to maneuver within a more open political system. Because direct presidential elections have not yet been held in Brazil, because the military retain so many prerogatives and powers, and because the actual civilian president, José Sarney, uses the military as a critical part of his power base, the Brazilian transition is in fact far from complete. Indeed, as I discuss in Chapter 7, some people question whether the "New Republic" that began in 1985 yet warrants classification as a democracy. In Brazil, not only was there little analysis of the role of the military in the transition, there was little public debate about how to demilitarize the polity in the future. Many people seemed to believe that with a civilian president, and with the former opposition party in control of the Congress, demilitarization of the polity would occur without an explicit strategy. It is now clear that this was a false expectation. Since a monopoly of the use of force is required for a modern democracy, failure to develop capacities to control the military represents an abdication of democratic power.

I HAVE BEEN thinking about the problems addressed in this book since November 1974 when I visited Brazil after the opposition scored impressive gains against the military-controlled party. In interviews with members of the opposition, and some of the key military strategists, I became convinced that a certain dialectic—which I have referred to as "regime concession and societal conquest"—had begun. I did not know then where it would lead, but I decided to follow it closely. In the ensuing years, I have been involved in numerous related projects that have informed my study in ways it is difficult to fully be aware of, much less adequately acknowledge.

In 1974, I began to discuss the process of authoritarian erosion with my colleague Juan Linz, who is a specialist on Spain and on modern authoritarianism. While we were still busy editing *The Breakdown of Democratic Regimes*, our conversations had begun to focus on problems of transition to democratic rule. Indeed, we concluded our 1978 preface to that project with the following words:

> High priority for further work along these lines should now be given to the analysis of the conditions that lead to the breakdown of authoritarian regimes, to the process of transition from authoritarian to democratic regimes, and especially to the polit-

ical dynamics of the consolidation of postauthoritarian democracies.[8]

To this end, we began by creating a course devoted to these themes. One of my grateful acknowledgments then is to Juan Linz, and to the many gifted and dedicated students at Yale and Columbia with whom it has been my privilege to work.

In the ensuing years, I have been a participant in four large collective projects that focus on different aspects of the question of the power of the modern state,[9] on the comparative analysis of transitions from authoritarian rule in Europe and Latin America,[10] on U.S. policies that all too often contributed to the emergence and prolongation of authoritarian regimes in Latin America,[11] and on social movements, political-economy, and democratic struggles in contemporary Brazil.[12] I consider all these issues extremely important; numerous publications have resulted from these projects to which I have contributed several papers. In this book, therefore, I concentrate quite specifically on the question of the military, while building and drawing upon the four previous projects.

Since 1978 I have visited Brazil at least once a year, and often more, to conduct research for this and other work. Since 1980 I

[8] Juan J. Linz and Alfred Stepan, eds., *The Breakdown of Democratic Regimes*, ix–x.

[9] The final product of this project was published as Peter Evans, Dietrich Rueschemeyer, and Theda Skocpol, eds., *Bringing the State Back In*. My contribution to that volume focused on patterns of resistance in civil society to authoritarian state power, "State Power and the Strength of Civil Society in the Southern Cone of Latin America."

[10] Guillermo O'Donnell, Philippe C. Schmitter, and Laurence Whitehead, eds., *Transitions from Authoritarian Rule*. My article in that volume is "Paths toward Redemocratization: Theoretical and Comparative Considerations."

[11] Cynthia Brown, ed., *With Friends Like These: The America's Watch Report on Human Rights and U.S. Policy in Latin America*, introduction by Alfred Stepan, preface by Jacobo Timmerman.

[12] Alfred Stepan, ed., *Democratizing Brazil: Problems of Transition and Consolidation*. I wrote *Rethinking Military Politics* at the same time I was editing *Democratizing Brazil*. I refer in the text to *Democratizing Brazil* as a "companion volume" because of the complementary nature of the two works.

have normally also visited Argentina, Uruguay, and Chile once a year. Working with colleagues of great quality, seriousness, originality, and generosity in these countries has been one of the formative experiences of my life. In Brazil I was fortunate to be a Tinker Fellow at the research institute CEBRAP where I first aired my research on comparative intelligence systems. Two fine scholars who were also opposition-party leaders, Fernando Henrique Cardoso and Francisco Weffort, greatly helped me to understand the intricacies of Brazilian politics. Bolivar Lamounier, Alexandre de S. C. Barros, David Fleischer, Paulo Sergio Pinheiro, and Maria do Carmo C. Souza cordially challenged and discussed my evidence and arguments. Two eminent journalist-editors and longtime friends, Elio Gaspari and Fernando Pedreira, gave my manuscripts an extremely close and critical reading. In Uruguay, the friendship and advice of social scientists Juan Rial, Luis Eduardo Gonzalez, and of Senator Jorge Batlle were of great help. In Argentina, Andrés Fontana of CEDES and I often conducted interviews together with political, military, and judicial actors involved in civil-military relations. The director of CEDES, Marcelo Cavarozzi, and I taught a course together at Yale from which I profited greatly. In Chile, Augusto Varas, Genaro Arriagada, Carlos Huneeus, Manuel Antonio Garretón, and Alejandro Foxley always generously shared insights and manuscripts.

Where possible, I cite in the text the more than two hundred participants in political parties, social movements, the church and, of course, the military organizations whom I interviewed. Long interviews with Raul Alfonsín of Argentina, Tancredo Neves of Brazil, and Eduardo Frei of Chile, while they were planning strategies of democratic opposition to the military, were of great importance. In Brazil, the two senior military leaders of the abertura, Ernesto Geisel and Golbery do Couto e Silva, gave me their arguments as to why they thought they had to initiate an opening of the authoritarian regime. In Uruguay, interviews with Julio María Sanguinetti and Hugo Medina gave me the perspective of the key party architect and the key military architect, respectively, of the "Naval Club Pact" that facilitated the Uruguayan transition. Through Juan Linz, I met at Yale the most critical political leader of the Spanish transition, Adolfo Suárez, and the central military figure, Gutiérrez Mellado.

A stay at the Latin American Center of St. Antony's College, Oxford University, as a Ford Fellow allowed me to discuss the early stages of this project with scholars from many countries in congenial and supportive surroundings.

In the United States, Jan Knippers Black, David Collier, J. Samuel Fitch, Juan Linz, Guillermo O'Donnell, and Peter Smith gave valuable critical support in reading the manuscript in various stages.

At Princeton University Press, Sandy Thatcher again played a vital and helpful role.

At different moments along the way, I was greatly assisted by my Graduate Research Assistants at Columbia University, Margaret Keck, Michael Fitzpatrick, Biorn Maybury-Lewis, Edward Gibson, and William Nylen.

My wife, historian Nancy Leys Stepan, as always, tried her British best to eliminate social science pomposity and jargon.

**Rethinking Military Politics**

# CHAPTER ONE

# Military Politics in Three
# Polity Arenas: Civil Society,
# Political Society, and the State

THE TITLE of this chapter is certainly ponderous, possibly pompous, but unfortunately necessary. The focus throughout this work is on military politics in the polity. I use the word "polity" to call attention to the classic Aristotelian concern with how people organize themselves for collective life in the polis.[1] For a modern polity in the midst of a democratization effort, it is conceptually and politically useful to distinguish three important arenas of the polity: civil society, political society, and the state. Obviously, in any given polity these three arenas expand and shrink at different rates, interpenetrate or even dominate each other, and constantly change.[2]

Very schematically, by "civil society" I mean that arena where manifold social movements (such as neighborhood associations, women's groups, religious groupings, and intellectual currents)

---

[1] For Aristotle's argument that there is an "imminent impulse in all men toward an association of this order," see *The Politics*, Book 1, Chapter 1, Sections 6–7, 14–15.

[2] Cardoso's article in the companion volume, *Democratizing Brazil*, ed. Alfred Stepan, is particularly rich in this respect. He shows how the great growth of the state enterprises has made them in some respects a part of civil society. He is also keenly aware of how civil and political groupings, in order to gain a greater degree of control over the state, must devise new practical and philosophical approaches to democratic collective actions within the state apparatus. Our two approaches are similar but are conducted on different levels of abstraction. One difference is that I insist, for reasons of analysis and political practice, on explicitly treating political society and civil society as distinct categories. He does so implicitly. My analysis in this book consciously sacrifices systematic attention to economic structures, both in order to highlight my discussion of the political aspects of the polity and because of their extensive coverage in the companion volume by Cardoso, Fishlow, Bacha, and Malan.

and civic organizations from all classes (such as lawyers, journalists, trade unions, and entrepreneurs) attempt to constitute themselves in an ensemble of arrangements so that they can express themselves and advance their interests.

By "political society" in a democratizing setting I mean that arena in which the polity specifically arranges itself for political contestation to gain control over public power and the state apparatus. At best, civil society can destroy an authoritarian regime. However, a full democratic transition must involve political society, and the composition and consolidation of a democratic polity must entail serious thought and action about those core institutions of a democratic political society—political parties, elections, electoral rules, political leadership, intraparty alliances, and legislatures—through which civil society can constitute itself politically to select and monitor democratic government.

By "the state" I mean something more than "government." It is the continuous administrative, legal, bureaucratic, and coercive system that attempts not only to manage the state apparatus but to structure relations *between* civil and public power and to structure many crucial relationships *within* civil and political society.[3]

In an extreme monist (or what some would call totalitarian) polity, the state eliminates any significant autonomy in political or civil society. In a strong authoritarian regime, political society is frequently absorbed by dominant groups into the state, but civil society characteristically has at least some spheres of autonomy.

I make these distinctions knowing full well that Gramsci, Hegel, Locke, Rousseau, and in the companion volume to this study, *Democratizing Brazil*, Cardoso and Weffort use different definitions. I think, however, that the strongest defense of a definition is its usefulness in analysis, and these working definitions may help illuminate some frequently obscured relationships within a democratizing polity like Brazil. Let us see.

In the democratizing period in Brazil between 1974 and 1985, the most popular topics of systematic, scholarly social science

[3] See my discussion in *The State and Society: Peru in Comparative Perspective*, especially the preface.

concerned new movements within civil society that presented challenges to the authoritarian state, such as the church, the new unionism, the new entrepreneurs, the press, the Association of Brazilian Lawyers, women's groups, and neighborhood associations. Because the changes in civil society were so significant, interesting, and normatively attractive, scholarly attention in more than fifty published works on these topics is quite understandable.[4] As Cardoso argues,

> In Brazilian political language, everything which was an organized fragment which escaped the immediate control of the authoritarian order was being designated *civil society*. Not rigorously, but effectively, the whole opposition . . . was being described as if it were the movement of Civil Society.[5]

"Civil society" became the political celebrity of the abertura. Politically the phrase had two tactical advantages in Brazilian discourse. First, because it explicitly was meant to entail opposition to the regime, the regime found it difficult to appropriate the meaning to its own advantage. Second, it created bonds between groups who in other settings were antagonists: São Paulo entrepreneurs and São Paulo metallurgical workers equally shared in the charismatic legitimacy of being part of the new "civil society."

The intense attention given to "civil" as opposed to "political" society was not without its strategic problems for the democratizing opposition. Important segments within the church and the new labor movement—two key segments of civil society—were deeply suspicious of "intermediaries" and "negotiations." They favored direct participation and articulation of demands, with the ideologically favored groups being "base" organizations. Partisans of this ideological current tended to be deeply suspicious of political parties. Opposition politicians in Congress—many of whom were seen as having been too tame during the pre-abertura period—were held in low esteem, and few organic links were

---

[4] See the ample references in the Keck, Mainwaring, Della Cava, and Alvarez articles in *Democratizing Brazil*.

[5] See his article in *Democratizing Brazil*.

forged between those opposition forces whose ideological and material resources were drawn from the arena of civil society and those opposition forces whose resources and style of action were associated with the arena of political society.

The military regime understood this sharp separation between the two arenas of the opposition and exploited the weakness. Again and again in the late 1970s and early 1980s the military altered the rules of the game for political society (physically and metaphorically isolated in Brasília and surrounded by the state). In this period civil society almost never came to the defense of political society. The regime's strategists were understandably happy with this pattern of behavior of the opposition that supported *liberalization* more than *democratization*.

This is a crucial distinction. In an authoritarian setting, "liberalization" may entail a mix of policy and social changes, such as less censorship of the media, somewhat greater working room for the organization of autonomous working-class activities, the reintroduction of some legal safeguards such as *habeas corpus* for individuals, the releasing of most political prisoners, the return of political exiles, possibly measures for improving the distribution of income, and, most important, the toleration of political opposition. "Democratization" entails liberalization but is a wider and more specifically political concept. Democratization requires open contestation for the right to win control of the government, and this in turn requires free elections, the results of which determine who governs. Using these definitions it is clear there can be liberalization without democratization. Liberalization refers fundamentally to civil society. Democratization involves civil society, but it refers fundamentally to political society.

There were also conceptual and analytical problems with a literature of the democratizing process that focused so heavily on civil society. Most scholars became specialists on the oppositional activity of specific fragments of civil society: base community specialists, new union specialists, specialists on lawyer associations, or the new entrepreneurs. This scholarly focus—though it produced some of the best and most exciting work on social movements anywhere in the world in the period—deflected attention from three important relationships.

First, it tended to leave understudied the immensely complex and innovative *horizontal relations of civil society with itself*, which helped interweave the weft and warp of civil society and give it a more variegated, more resistant fabric.[6]

Second, insufficient analytical attention was given to the problem of how the gap between the opposition based in the civil arena and opposition based in the political arena could be bridged.

Third, there were hundreds of scholarly and newspaper articles with titles such as "Entrepreneurs Against the State," "The Church Against the State," and "Metalworkers Against the State." However, this unidirectional vertical perspective led to a serious neglect, not only of the inter- and intraclass horizontal linkages, but also of the internal contradictions within the state (especially within the military) that led fractions of the state apparatus to seek out (and to tolerate the partial empowerment of) allies within civil society. Thus, even the analysis of the growth of civil society is impoverished if the state's *downward reach* for new allies in civil society is not documented descriptively and incorporated conceptually.[7]

Because civil society was the celebrity of the abertura and the prevailing discourse privileged the dichotomy ("Civil Society versus the State"), activists and scholars alike tended to belittle the role of parties, Congress, and elections, and "political society" was relatively neglected in the literature. Nonetheless, there were at least a score of solid books and articles in addition to a well-conceived collective longitudinal election project that focused precisely on political society in the democratizing period.[8]

[6] There is a great story waiting to be told. I discuss and document part of this innovative horizontal process in my "State Power and the Strength of Civil Society in the Southern Cone of Latin America." The subject, however, deserves book-length treatment.

[7] I analyze this "downward reach" in Chapter 3.

[8] For an analysis of the neglect of political society—especially the role of the opposition in elections—as well as a discussion of the solid literature on parties and elections, see Bolivar Lamounier, " 'Authoritarian Brazil' Revisited." La-

Let us now turn to the question of the state, and specifically to the military as a part of the authoritarian state apparatus. As late as mid-1984, although the Brazilian opening was over ten years old, to my knowledge there was not even *one* systematic academic social science monograph or thesis in Portuguese or English, about the military in the period of distensão and abertura.[9]

Clearly, both for theoretical and empirical reasons, if the analytic focus is on the transition to democracy—especially a transi-

mounier played an important role throughout the democratizing period in developing research and discussion on political society.

[9] I called attention to this point in my "O Que Estão Pensando os Militares." The major exception to this neglect is the article by Eliezer Rizzo de Oliveira, "Conflits militaires et décisions sous la présidence du Général Geisel (1974–1979)." Also see Jan Knippers Black, "The Military and Political Decompression in Brazil." There are some important comparative reflections in Alexandre de Souza Costa Barros and Edmundo Coelho, "Military Intervention and Withdrawal in South America."

The standard works on the modern Brazilian military focus on the period *before* the abertura. See Alexandre de Souza Costa Barros, "The Brazilian Military: Professional Socialization, Political Performance and State Building"; Edmundo Campos Coelho, *Em Busca de Identidade: O Exército e a Política na Sociedade Brasileira*; Eurico de Lima Figueiredo, *Os Militares e a Democracia: Análise Estrutural da Ideologia do Golpe. Castelo Branco*; René Armand Dreifuss, *1964: A Conquista do Estado, Açaõ Política, Poder e Golpe de Classe*; Alfred Stepan, *The Military in Politics*; and Alfred Stepan, "The "New Professionalism of Internal Warfare and Military Role Expansion."

The best systematic, empirically based publication on the security apparatus as it functioned in the abertura period focused exclusively on the military police of São Paulo. See the excellent study by Paulo Sérgio Pinheiro, "Polícia e Crise Política: O Caso das Polícias Militares."

For the military in the abertura period, three books written from a journalistic vantage point provide some of the most important leads and perspectives. See Walder de Góes, *O Brasil do General Geisel: Estudo do Processo de Tomada de Decisão no Regime Militar-Burocrático*; André Gustavo Stumpf and Merval Pereira Filho, *A Segunda Guerra: Sucessão de Geisel*; and Bernardo Kucinski, *Abertura, a História de uma Crise*.

Four works with valuable material on the military in the abertura that appeared in 1983–1985 are Maria Helena Moreira Alves, *Estado e Oposição no Brasil (1964–1984)*; René Armand Dreifuss and Otávio Soares Dulci, "As Forças Armadas e a Política"; Walder de Góes, "O Novo Regime Militar no Brasil"; and Wilfred Bacchus, "Long-Term Military Rulership in Brazil: Ideologic Consensus and Dissensus, 1963–1983."

tion that is occurring within the specific context of a military-led authoritarian regime—the military component itself must be studied.

What explains this stunning neglect of the military? Part of the explanation is an understandable fear of repression and censorship. However, it should be noted that this same period saw the publication of numerous detailed accounts of torture in particular, and harshly critical books about the authoritarian regime in general. Certainly, it is also relatively difficult for scholars to do research on the military, especially if they are Brazilian citizens; however, the Brazilian military annually publishes a considerable quantity of documents that merit content analysis and many retired colonels and generals have been surprisingly willing to talk to journalists. Part of the explanation for neglect would seem therefore to be normative disdain for the military as a topic (the obverse of the normative attraction to new groups in civil society). This is a longstanding problem, often referred to as "the liberal bias." It probably merits calling attention once again to Max Weber's eminently sound, if neglected, dictum in his famous essay on science as a vocation, "the primary task of a useful teacher is to teach his students to recognize 'inconvenient' facts—I mean the facts that are inconvenient for their party opinions."[10]

Finally, a significant part of the neglect of the military as a central topic of empirical research, in my judgment, has its origins in theory. The 1970s witnessed a worldwide boom in theoretical writings about the state. Probably the single most influential theorist of the state was Poulantzas, an advocate of the "relative autonomy of the state." However, his analysis of the reasons for state autonomy has nothing to do with his analysis of empirically observed dynamics of state bureaucracies, but rather derives from his *functionalist assumption* that such a degree of autonomy is a structural requirement of capital accumulation and domination in an advanced capitalist state.[11] Note how little autonomous power

[10] Max Weber, "Science as a Vocation," in *From Max Weber: Essays in Sociology*, ed. H. H. Gerth and C. Wright Mills, 147.

[11] Nicos Poulantzas, especially in his *Political Power and Social Classes*, is primarily a functionalist, notwithstanding the rich problems he raises. For a pointed discussion of the empirical and theoretical questions begged by such func-

bureaucracies are accorded in his theoretical framework; for him the state is "the site of organization of the dominant class in the relationship to the dominated classes. It is a *site* and a *center* of the exercise of power, but it possesses no power of its own."[12] Politics and political science are about power. What is particularly revealing about the Poulantzas quotation is that the theoretical logic of his form of diffuse structural determinism conceptually *removes* the military from the exercise of power.[13] This theoretical perspective is misleading. Any military organization is of course affected by the overall balance of class power within which it functions. However, it is also true that any large complex organization has some institutional interests of its own and prerogatives its members seek to advance, as well as some changes or outcomes in the overall political system that it, more than other organizations, particularly fears and thus resists. Complex organizations thus have interests and capacities to advance their interests.

When the unit of analysis is not just a complex organization, but a military organization such as the one found in Brazil from 1964 until 1985—which supplied the bulk of the coercive resources of the state, from whose membership the head of state was selected, and from which a significant portion of the most important state enterprises' and agencies' heads were selected—the requirement to study the specific organizational structures and norms of that military organization is powerful.

The argument becomes overwhelming when we realize that both in 1964 and in 1969–1971 there were "Brumairean moments" during which strategic fractions of the bourgeoisie were fearful enough to abdicate, in essence, to the military their claims to rule, in return for the coercive protection they thought only

---

tionalism, see Anthony Giddens, *A Contemporary Critique of Historical Materialism*, 214–217; and Douglas C. Bennett and Kenneth E. Sharpe, "The State as Banker and as Entrepreneur: The Last Resort Character of the Mexican State's Economic Intervention, 1917–1970."

[12] Nicos Poulantzas, *State, Power, Socialism*, 148. Poulantzas's emphasis.

[13] For a brilliant analysis of precisely this problem by a political philosopher, see Stephen Lukes, *Power: A Radical View*, 52–56.

the military could give them.[14] Here the emphasis of Poulantzas is again misleading. Power does of course diffusely reside in structures, but it can also be actively exercised by individuals controlling complex organizations. Fear may create a social base and the Brumairean moment. But as the São Paulo entrepreneurs learned in the late 1970s, the receding of bourgeois fear does not mean that power once yielded to the military will be given back without a struggle.[15] In the study of the military, as in the study of any other complex organization, we must also bear in mind the ratchet effect of bureaucratic momentum and aggrandizement.

Antonio Gramsci and Max Weber, working from very different theoretical and normative perspectives, both understood the central role of the coercive apparatus in modern, especially authoritarian, states. Gramsci, on various occasions, asserts that "domination" is a function of *hegemony* and *coercion*. He refers in one place to hegemony as "the spontaneous consent given by the great masses of the population to the general direction imposed on social life by the dominant fundamental group."[16] For Gramsci, to the extent that such hegemony does not exist in civil society, compliance is obtained by "the apparatus of state coercive power which 'legally' enforces discipline on those groups who do not 'consent' either actively or passively."[17] In the case of Brazil—especially in the period 1964–1974—we are dealing with what O'Donnell calls a "bureaucratic-authoritarian" regime, or what I have called an "exclusionary" authoritarian regime. Whatever it

[14] Karl Marx, in "The Eighteenth Brumaire of Louis Bonaparte," described as one of the characteristics of the Bonapartist regime the abdication by the bourgeoisie of its right to rule in exchange for other kinds of protection by the ensuing strong state. Here, I use the word "Brumairean" to evoke the kind of relation described in Marx's essay.

[15] See Eli Diniz and Renato Boschi, *Empresariado Nacional e Estado no Brasil*; Luis Carlos Bresser Pereira, *O Colapso de uma Aliança de Classes*; and Fernando Henrique Cardoso, "O Papel dos Empresários no Processo de Transição: O Caso Brasileiro."

[16] Antonio Gramsci, *Selections from the Prison Notebooks*, ed. Quintin Hoare and Geoffrey Nowell Smith, 12.

[17] Ibid.

is labeled, the Brazilian authoritarian regime at no time came remotely close to achieving Gramscian hegemony.[18]

Another major conceptual approach to the state, Max Weber's, also put great emphasis on the role of domination and the physical and organizational means of domination. He explicitly says "the state is a relation of men dominating men" and that "organized domination, which calls for continuous administration, requires that human conduct be conditioned to obedience . . . towards those masters who claim to be the bearers of legitimate power. On the other hand, by virtue of this obedience, organized domination requires the control of those material goods which in a given case are necessary for the use of physical violence."[19] In the context of an authoritarian state such as Brazil, a serious reading of Gramsci or Weber would require specific attention to the coercive apparatus, that is, the military and the security community. They were, after all, the "inconvenient facts" of the abertura.

However, it is also a theoretical and empirical imperative to then locate this institutional analysis within the larger context of *power as a relationship*. A dynamic, contextually sensitive analysis of the movement from a strong military-led authoritarian regime to the transition to democracy entails the assessment of power relationships between three interactive, but conceptually distinct, arenas of the polity: civil society, political society, and the state. I will attempt to use all these concepts in the ensuing relational analysis of power changes.

[18] Guillermo O'Donnell, *Modernization and Bureaucratic-Authoritarianism: Studies in South American Politics*; and Stepan, *State and Society*, where, in Chapter 3, I argued that the Mexican authoritarian regime had a substantial degree of Gramscian hegemony and contrasted this sharply with the Brazilian authoritarian regime.

[19] See "Politics as a Vocation," in *From Max Weber*, 78, 80. I discuss Weber's theory of the state in my *State and Society*, xi–xiv.

# CHAPTER TWO

# The Brazilian Intelligence System in Comparative Perspective

AN UNDERSTANDING of the organizational prerogatives and spheres of autonomy of the military and intelligence components of the state apparatus throws light on why splits in the state apparatus are often a precondition for the erosion of an authoritarian regime, and why political and civil society must normally devise new strategies for empowering themselves to monitor and control military and intelligence systems if new democracies are to be consolidated.

The Brazilian case is especially important in comparative terms because the intelligence system became more autonomous than in any other modern authoritarian regime in Latin America; because liberalization began within the state apparatus owing to the contradictions generated by the increasing autonomy of the security apparatus; and because the initial path to liberalization via internal change from above left dangerous legacies in the form of continued prerogatives that are inconsistent with full redemocratization.

In a previous work I argued that shifts in the content of military professionalism were contributing to an authoritarian expansion of what the military conceived to be their role in the polity. My interpretation contrasted with the then widely held view that increased professionalism would lead to an apolitical military. I contrasted two ideal types of professionalisms as shown in Table 2.1.

Subsequent events have strengthened the argument.[1] Certainly,

---

[1] See Joseph Comblin, *A Ideologia da Segurança Nacional: O Poder Militar na América Latina*. For a comparative analysis, with extensive citations, of military ideology in the four bureaucratic-authoritarian regimes, see Genaro Arriagada Herrera, *El Pensamiento Político de los Militares (Estudios Sobre Chile, Argentina, Brasil y Uruguay)*. For Uruguay, the most useful primary texts are the two massive books published by the Junta de Comandantes en Jefe, *La Subversión* and *El Pro-*

as Guillermo O'Donnell has stressed, there were very important structural components to the emergence of bureaucratic-authoritarian regimes in South America.[2] However, close analysis of the emergence and operation of these regimes also underscores the fact that "new professionalism" (or what others such as Joseph Comblin and Manuel Antonio Garretón have called the "national security" state ideology) figured prominently in the military's self-justification of their vastly expanded role in politics. In addition to Brazil (especially in 1968–1973), sweepingly repressive regimes of this type were inaugurated in Chile and Uruguay in 1973 and in Argentina in 1976. The central role of the new professional/national security ideology in the rationalization of all these regimes has by now been amply documented and need not be discussed further here.

How far did the security community dominance go in Brazil, especially in comparison to the other three bureaucratic authoritarian regimes in Argentina, Chile, and Uruguay? Here the story is rather complex. If we are assessing the percentage of people killed by the state in the act and aftermath of taking power, Chile in 1973–1974 ranks the highest. If we are assessing the percentage of people who disappeared as a result of the action of hydra-headed and decentralized security forces, before and after taking power, Argentina in 1975–1979 ranks the highest. If we are evaluating the percentage of the population that was detained, interrogated, and intimidated by the security forces, Uruguay ranks the highest (and came the closest, especially in 1975–1979, to having the feel of a totalitarian state). However, if we ask in which country did the peak intelligence organization achieve the highest level

ceso Político. For Chile in comparative perspective, see "La Ideología de Seguridad Nacional en los Régimenes Militares," in Augusto Varas, Felipe Agüero, and Fernando Bustamente, Chile, Democracia, Fuerzas Armadas. Their book has a bibliographic category for national security doctrine within the Chilean military with fifty-eight entries. For Brazil, many valuable references are contained in Moreira Alves, Estado e Oposição no Brasil (1964–1984). For Argentina, see O'Donnell, Modernization and Bureaucratic-Authoritarianism.

[2] O'Donnell, Modernization and Bureaucratic-Authoritarianism.

TABLE 2.1. Contrasting Paradigms: The Old Professionalism of External Defense, the New Professionalism of Internal Security and National Development

|  | Old Professionalism | New Professionalism |
|---|---|---|
| Function of military | External security | Internal security |
| Civilian attitudes toward government | Civilians accept legitimacy of government | Segments of society challenge government legitimacy |
| Military skills required | Highly specialized skills incompatible with political skills | Highly interrelated political and military skills |
| Scope of military professional action | Restricted | Unrestricted |
| Impact of professional socialization | Renders the military politically neutral | Politicizes the military |
| Impact on civil-military relations | Contributes to an apolitical military and civilian control | Contributes to military-political managerialism and role expansion |

Source: Stepan, "The New Professionalism of Internal Warfare and Military Role-Expansion," in Stepan, ed., *Authoritarian Brazil* (New Haven: Yale University Press, 1973), 52.

of statutory-based role expansion and nonpersonalistic institution-alization within the state apparatus, there is no question that the answer is Brazil.[3]

Less than three months after the military regime took hold in Brazil, the Serviço Nacional de Informações (National Informa-

[3] Brazil's closest rival was Chile.

tion Service, hereafter referred to by its Portuguese initials, SNI) was created. The Decree Law that created the SNI gave it the following functions and prerogatives.[4]

1. The SNI is the organ of the president.
2. The goal of the SNI is to supervise and coordinate, in all the national territory, activities of information and counterinformation with particular reference to national security.
3. The SNI is to advise the president of matters pertaining to national security including the activities of ministries, state enterprises and parastatal organizations.
4. The SNI is to create the Sistema Nacional de Informações (National System of Information) and to arrange the necessary connections with state governors, private enterprises, and municipal administrations.
5. The SNI is to collect, evaluate, and integrate information and, furthermore, to act as staff to the National Security Council and to coordinate the planning activities of the secretary-general of the NSC.
6. The SNI is to promote the diffusion of necessary information to the government ministries.

General Golbery do Couto e Silva, the chief author of the decree and the first director of the SNI, later lamented that he had created a "monster." It is obvious, however, that regardless of its later expansion, the SNI was, from its inception, a powerful body.

From late 1968 until early 1972 Brazil witnessed a period of urban, and some rural, guerrilla resistance, and the hard-line tendency within the Brazilian military became much stronger. On December 13, 1968, the hard-line commanders imposed the harshest military coup in Brazilian history when they decreed the Fifth Institutional Act, closed the Congress, censored the press, and took away the political rights of—and even imprisoned—key leaders of civil and political society. This was the period of the most extensive torture and the most intense centralized and decentralized repression by the security forces. The director of the SNI for part

---

[4] Decree Law 4341, June 13, 1964.

of this period was General Emílio Garrastazú Médici. Throughout Médici's later presidency of Brazil (1969–1974) the functions and prerogatives of the sni grew.

General Golbery's initial idea had been to create a civil-military organ in which active-duty military were in the minority. In the original statute no official in the sni had to be drawn from the active-duty military. In 1964 none of the top six figures was an active-duty general; one, Golbery, was a retired general.[5] However, by late 1968, as the guerrilla conflict began and the hard line triumphed, the sni became militarized. Starting in late 1968, and extending throughout the duration of the regime, the six top sni posts were held by army generals still eligible for promotion.[6] The sni began as an agency for the gathering, coordinating, and evaluating of intelligence, but without a large, independent field operating staff.[7] From 1968 on, it increasingly came to be the country's fourth (albeit nonuniformed) service. The distinction is not irrelevant in the normal functioning of intelligence bodies. For example, in the United States the National Security Council (nsc) is the major advisory body on security issues to the president, but it does not control a large body of personnel. Its staff consists of approximately 175 people, including secretarial personnel.[8]

[5] Interview with General Golbery, September 15, 1981, in Brasília.

[6] Interviews with various sni officials and confirmed by newspaper accounts that gave the names and ranks of all key individuals in the sni. Note that the only top position in the sni that by statute must go to a military officer is the directorship of the Escola Nacional de Informações (esni). Decree Law 68 448, Art. 3 (March 31, 1971). In my interview with him (São Paulo, March 28, 1982), the first director of esni, General Enio dos Santos Pinheiro (ret.), said that the reason the director of esni must be an active-duty military officer is that one of the functions of the school is to train military attachés.

[7] Interview with Colonel Newton Leitão (ret.), in Rio de Janeiro in June 1982. Colonel Leitão was one of the four top officials in the sni when it was established in 1964.

[8] For the organizational structure of the nsc as it existed under the Carter presidency, see "Annex III: The nsc Staff and Organization, 1977–1981," in Zbigniew Brzezinski, *Power and Principle: Memoirs of the National Security Adviser, 1977–1981*, 570–573. For an excellent analysis of the various roles and organizational structures taken on by the nsc under every president from Truman to Carter, see Mark M. Lowenthal, "The National Security Council: Organizational History."

By 1971 the SNI was authorized to open its own school, the Escola Nacional da Informação (ESNI). When this school opened in 1973 all other advanced intelligence courses in Brazil were closed, including those at the Escola Superior de Guerra (ESG), which originally had been the institutional base of the more softline military such as President Castello Branco. In two interviews with General Enio dos Santos Pinheiro, the first commandant of the ESNI, he described to me the following ways in which the ESNI differed from the ESG after 1973. The ESNI had a permanent body of researchers; the ESG no longer did. The ESNI dealt with concrete case studies and real facts and was linked to an operating agency, whereas the ESG tended to formulate abstract doctrine and had no operational links. The ESNI ran a professional school, with four different sequences, which trained all candidates for the national intelligence system, administered tests, and taught English, Spanish, Russian, German, French, Italian, and eventually Arabic, whereas the ESG, in his judgment, ran a cross between an orientation course and a university extension course.[9] Clearly, within the intrastate arena the ESNI was accumulating powerful resources.

The new professionalism of internal security and national development in Brazil eventually produced a National Intelligence System that in formal terms monopolized more functions than any other major polity in the world and, unlike virtually any other major intelligence system, had no system of routine oversight short of the head of state. Before the distensão began in 1974, the official security apparatus in Brazil had the following formal characteristics, which (without even considering its very important informal characteristics) gave the security community substantial autono-

---

The present Brazilian conception of a "National Security Council" is indeed quite different. A discussion of the organization, composition, and role of the Brazilian National Security Council vis-à-vis the president, higher military commands, and the Congress in the post-1964 period may be found in C. Neale Ronning and Henry H. Keith, "Shrinking Political Arena," esp. 230–241.

[9] Interviews with General Enio dos Santos Pinheiro (ret.), in São Paulo, March 28 and June 15, 1982. Note that in a subsequent interview with a colonel who had attended the ESG and later held a key position at the ESNI, all of these distinctions were reiterated.

mous power within the state apparatus itself, as well as power to help the security community shape important parameters of civil and political society.

1. The SNI was the top domestic intelligence agency and the top international intelligence agency.

2. The head of the SNI was *de jure* a Cabinet minister and *de facto* a member of the inner cabinet with direct and daily access to the president.

3. The SNI had an official monopoly on advanced intelligence training; its school trained both military and civilians, including officials of the state and municipal organizations of the federal system, as well as many large parastatal and even large private organizations.

4. The SNI was independent and had its own agents in the field and thus its own operational capacity; for a broad range of activities, it did not have to rely on other agencies to operate.

5. The SNI, by law, maintained an office in every ministry, state enterprise, and university. The regional branches of the SNI maintained similar offices in the state organizations. The functions of these offices were (a) to examine all material of any importance; (b) to examine the security implications of any policy; (c) to screen all personnel with any degree of responsibility. The minister could, however, if he were supported by the president, overrule the SNI veto of any appointment of personnel he made.

6. The Central Agency within the SNI was responsible for internal security, strategic information, and special operations. It therefore coordinated not only all activities of the SNI itself but also the external intelligence activities of the other intelligence branches of the state, in particular the intelligence branches of the armed forces. The Central Agency combined the functions of coordination and liaison. The intelligence community in its entirety was called the Sistema Nacional de Informações (SISNI, National Intelligence System).

7. There was no permanent review agency (legislative or executive). The law simply stated that the SNI was an organ of the President of the Republic (Decree Law 55194, Chap. 2, Art. 2) and that personnel were to be approved annually by the president (Art. 18).

If we compare this combination of prerogatives with countries such as England, France, and the United States, we note striking differences. Not a single top intelligence agency in these latter three countries enjoys more than two of the seven bureaucratic prerogatives given the SNI. For example, all three countries have different agencies for domestic and external intelligence. In England, the peak domestic agency is the MI5, the peak external one, MI6. In France, the principal domestic agency is the DST, while the chief external agency is the DGSE. In the United States the chief domestic agency is the FBI, and the CIA is the chief external agency. None of the heads of these six agencies today has ministerial status. President Reagan appointed the head of the CIA, William J. Casey, to the Cabinet, but in the aftermath of the ''Iran-Contra'' affair, his successor, William Webster, pledged that he would avoid politics and not serve in the Cabinet. The head of the NSC in the United States (the Assistant to the President for National Security Affairs) may—depending upon the operating style of a particular president—enjoy informal Cabinet status and report to the president daily; but his tasks are primarily ones of coordination, planning and evaluation, and he supervises a relatively small staff with no permanent field operatives of its own. Lieutenant Colonel Oliver L. North violated both the spirit and the letter of the law by his ''Iran-Contra'' operations. None of the six peak agencies is allowed SNI's degree of routine statutorily sanctioned penetration into municipal and parastatal offices. Most importantly, all have permanent review agencies.[10]

Even if we examine intelligence agencies in the USSR (which I

[10] For information on the oversight and control of British intelligence agencies, see the series of articles by Duncan Campbell in *The New Statesman*, October 29, November 19, and November 26, 1982; plus Michael R. D. Foot, ''Britain—In-

realize have greater technical capacity and probably even greater political power relative to the SNI), we see that they have a more complex organizational structure of reporting and oversight. In the USSR, there are two peak agencies, the KGB (Committee for State Security) and the GRU (Chief Intelligence Directorate, or "Military Intelligence"). Both are responsible for internal and external intelligence. The chairman of the KGB is chosen by the dozen or so members of the Politburo. (Though it is not a part of the Soviet government, the Political Bureau of the Central Committee of the Communist Party of the Soviet Union is the supreme decision-making body in the CPSU, and thus in the Soviet Union.) The chairman reports to the Politburo through the USSR Council of Ministers (the Soviet government's highest administrative body), unless the KGB chairman is himself a Politburo member, in which case he reports directly. This practice varies as no ministry or individual other than the secretary-general of the CPSU—not Foreign Affairs, nor KGB, nor Defense—is entitled to an ex officio seat on the Politburo. Yuri Andropov, for example, as Brezhnev's KGB chairman, attained full-member status only after an extended period as a candidate member. Andropov's successor, Fedorchuk, did not attain such status as head of the KGB, while the incumbent, Chebrikov, did so rather shortly after his assumption of the post. Assignments and promotions within the KGB are screened by the

---

telligence Services." See also Crispin Aubrey, *Who's Watching You? Britain's Security Services and the Official Secrets Act.*

For France, see Roger Faligot and Pascal Krop, *La Piscine: Les services secrets français, 1944–1984*; and Jean-Pierre Marichy, "The Central Organization of Defense in France."

Extensive treatments of the composition, organization, activities management, and oversight of the U.S. intelligence community are to be found variously in Mark M. Lowenthal, *U.S. Intelligence: Evolution and Anatomy*; Jeffrey T. Richelson, *The U.S. Intelligence Community*; Scott D. Breckinridge, *The CIA and the U.S. Intelligence System*; John M. Oseth, *Regulating U.S. Intelligence Operations: A Study in Definition of the National Interest*; and Tyrus G. Fain, ed., *The Intelligence Community: History, Organization and Issues*. Also see Mark M. Lowenthal, "The National Security Council: Organizational History"; and his "The Central Intelligence Agency: Organizational History." Perhaps the most useful single volume covering the particulars of military intelligence is Gerald W. Hopple and Bruce W. Watson, eds., *The Military Intelligence Community*.

Administrative Organs Department of the Central Committee Secretariat (as they are for the Ministries of Internal Affairs and Defense, as well). The department secretary himself is selected by the Party Central Committee. The GRU, as but one of eleven departments of the Soviet (armed forces) General Staff, reports to the chief of the General Staff, who in turn reports to the Main Military Council (which has responsibility for the administering of policy and the integration/coordination of the forces within the Defense Ministry). Military intelligence policy (and defense policy generally) is formulated by the Defense Council, composed of party (Politburo), government (Council of Ministers), and military (Ministry of Defence) leaders. The GRU also reports directly to the KGB; nonetheless, it is seen as providing party leaders with a valuable second viewpoint on many issues.[11]

It seems that the SNI—the most institutionally elaborated expression in Brazil of the logic of new professionalism—stands out from among its counterparts in the world in several respects, particularly with regard to its near monopoly in operations and training, the right under law for the director of the Service to sit on the Cabinet, and the right under the law to have an official office in every government department, state enterprise, and university which can inspect the daily workings of the administrative machinery. In addition, it appears to act as its own liaison, coordination, and review body. Democratic countries, on the other hand, attempt to achieve some control over the secret services by proliferation and separation of intelligence units, obliging them to operate through other agencies in a legal capacity, controlling their access to the chief executive, and differentiating the functions of reporting, coordination, liaison, and review. By such means the intelligence agencies face a variety of countervailing powers and mechanisms that are designed to control the normal tendency of intelligence agencies to seek greater autonomy. However, the sole major, institutionalized means of control over the

---

[11] See Jeffrey T. Richelson, *Sword and Shield: The Soviet Intelligence and Security Apparatus*, esp. 21–67 and 229–260; and Robert H. Baker, "Central Organizations of Defense in the Soviet Union."

SNI is the president's right to annual review of all personnel; this is not negligible, although its substantive impact is unknown.

## PEAK INTELLIGENCE ORGANIZATIONS IN URUGUAY, ARGENTINA, AND CHILE

The new professional logic, especially as regards institutionalized and legal prerogatives of the peak intelligence organization, went much further in Brazil than in the other three bureaucratic-authoritarian regimes of Uruguay, Argentina, and Chile. In particular, the national security state and the SNI became embedded in the normal institutionalized routine of the state apparatus to a degree not found in the other three countries.

In Uruguay, ESEDENA (the would-be equivalent of ESG) was not even founded until five years after the military assumed power in 1973, and it was closed for reorganization in 1986. Thus, "new professionalism" in Uruguay did not have the extensive foundation in the military educational and socialization system found in Brazil. The intelligence community did play a major role in the campaign against the Tupamaro guerrillas, but intelligence was defined mainly as operational and was developed and controlled by combat units of the armed forces who exchanged information with each other on a lateral basis. In interviews, two of the senior Uruguayan military officials involved in political-military affairs both said that a conscious decision was made to rotate *all* officers into and out of intelligence duties in order to, first, familiarize them with the vital tasks of intelligence, and second, avoid the creation of an autonomous intelligence service. Thus, they did not create a school such as ESNI to centralize intelligence training— precisely because there were no full-time career specialists in intelligence. Nonetheless, even after the military in Uruguay had accepted in principle a return to civilian power, three areas of conflict existed between the military and the returning democratic parties. As late as 1984 military leaders argued openly that (1) intelligence was a critical factor, and they must maintain control of this domain; (2) they had greater power than the political parties, and reserved the right to intervene in the future if necessary; and (3) the politicians should accept some form of institutionalized military presence in a newly created National Security Council as the price of military extrication. Even though the Uruguayan military ceded many of their prerogatives after the first year of civilian rule, the intelligence system retained greater size and operational capacities—and a greater focus on "domestic subversion"—than it had in the early 1960s.[12]

In Argentina the abuse by decentralized intelligence services in the 1975–1978 period was notorious, and I do not want for an instant to minimize the impact of intelligence groups on civil and political society. However, three factors precluded the emergence of any unified national service comparable to the SNI. First, General Teófilo Goyret, a director in 1976–1977 of Argentina's equivalent of the ESG, the Escuela de Defensa Nacional, argues that the Escuela and the mini-SNI (first called Control de Estado, and later SIDE) were born under mixed stars because both were founded by Perón and have always been controversial and lacked prestige in some key military circles. He had attended the Brazilian ESG and was familiar with the SNI and the ESNI and insisted that Argentina had nothing comparable.[13] Second, the 1976 decision to divide power between the president and the Junta, and to divide national, provincial and parastatal posts within the Junta on a one-third army, one-third navy, and one-third air force basis, implied a great *de facto* fractionalization of organizational power that inhib-

---

[12] This paragraph is based on interviews with the first head of ESEDENA, Director General José Luis Ramagli, and with members of his faculty at ESEDENA in Montevideo, September 28 and October 1, 1981, with Colonel Jorge Martínez, the chief staff aide to the Commission of Political Affairs (COMASPO) of the Combined General Staff, and with the chief of operations (G-3) of the Uruguayan Army in the same period. For an overview of civil-military affairs in the first years of Uruguay's bureaucratic-authoritarian regime, see, François Lerin and Cristina Torres, *Les Transformations institutionelles de l'Uruguay (1973–1977)*. See the "Pacto del Club Naval" that the armed forces, the Partido Colorado, and the Frente Amplio agreed to as the rules of the game for military exit, reprinted in Juan Rial, "Las Reglas del Juego Electoral en Uruguay y sus Implicaciones." For my documentation and a more extensive assessment of the role of the Uruguayan intelligence community after the transition to democracy, see Chapter 7.

[13] Interview in Buenos Aires on July 26, 1982.

ited the emergence of an all-powerful, nationally integrated intelligence system. Third, in Brazil the army completely dominated the other two services, and the SNI had a special relationship to the army. In Argentina the navy was a serious competitor to the army and would have contested army control of any SNI.[14] This much greater fragmentation of the Argentine state apparatus during the military regime is distinctive in itself, but it is also part of an enduring long-term contrast with the more historically unified Brazilian state apparatus.

In Chile the national intelligence service is extremely powerful. However, it is less explicitly institutionalized, and less a factor of independent (as opposed to derived) power. Three things are clear. One, the Chilean regime is much more personalistic than that of Brazil. Two, DINA, and even more its successor CNI, are seen more as the personal extension of the president than as a permanent part of the state apparatus. And finally, two of the three Brazilian presidents between 1969 and 1984 had as their original power base their direction of the SNI. In Chile, given Pinochet's monopoly of the presidency, neither DINA nor the CNI has yet played a role in the selection of military presidents.

## BRAZIL: THE GROWING AUTONOMY OF THE INTELLIGENCE APPARATUS

We can conclude therefore that the Brazilian SNI had an extraordinary degree of legally sanctioned prerogatives and bureaucratic autonomy found neither in other democracies nor in the other bureaucratic-authoritarian regimes. Power, however, is derived not only from formal statutes. I argued in Chapter 1 that complex organizations normally have interests they want to advance and those they want to impede. The SNI clearly had both. Let me mention three of the most obvious. First, throughout the Brazilian authoritarian regime there was a rotation of presidents, all of whom

---

[14] For a detailed discussion of the division of posts, see the unsigned article, "La Cúpula Cívico-Militar," *Carta Política* (May 1976), 32–35; and Jorge Reinaldo Vanossi, "Reflexiones Sobre el Nuevo Régimen Institucional Argentino."

came from within the army. There thus existed the permanent possibility that SNI officials could use the intelligence apparatus to advance their own personal prospects, or to impede the presidential candidacy or military promotions of those who were perceived to be hostile to the SNI's prerogatives and policies. Democratization would curtail their privileged positions in the power-brokering process. Second, during Brazil's guerrilla conflicts of 1969–1972, units and individuals associated with the security forces tortured and killed numbers of citizens, and thus acquired an institutional interest in blocking liberalization of the press or giving greater autonomy to the legal system where charges could be pressed. Third, the rank and file of the SNI—even if they were military men receiving special allowances—wore civilian clothes, and often had special access to cars, planes, and personal budgets. They thus had a predictable material interest in sustaining the bureaucratic routines of the authoritarian state that underwrote these privileges—privileges that most of the active-duty military, as well as civilians, resented.

The Brazilian situation was complicated by another phenomenon. So far we have simply been analyzing the peak national intelligence organization, the SNI. However, Brazil, especially in 1967–1972, saw the emergence of numerous other intelligence organizations. In 1967, amid internal debate about the danger of assuming police functions and creating parallel chains of command, the army created a Centro de Informações do Exército (CIE), which was not a part of the army General Staff but rather reported directly to the Minister of the Army. Only in 1970, in the middle of the antiguerrilla struggle, did the office become fully staffed and operational. In 1970 the air force restructured its own intelligence service and created a Centro de Informações (CISA), which was similar to CIE.

Via a series of informal mechanisms in São Paulo beginning in 1968, there emerged a unified antiguerrilla force called Operação Bandeirantes (OBAN), which received private and public monies. By the early 1970s, the OBAN system was institutionalized. Each military region had an overall office, called Centro de Operações de Defesa Interna (CODI), to integrate intelligence operations. Regardless of the specific seniority of the army, navy, or air force commanders in the region, the CODI was placed under the jurisdiction of the G-2 of a regional army command, such as the Second Army in São Paulo. The formula in essence gave the army authority over the navy and the air force in regard to internal-security matters. In one respect it was a step toward overcoming the growing anarchy within the Brazilian military. The Minister of the Army, Orlando Geisel, attempted to reinstate military order by acting as *de facto* Minister of Defense. However, the new system produced its own contradictions.

The CODI had no operatives. The actual operational group for intelligence and antisubversive activities in a military region such as São Paulo were located in the offices of a Destacamento de Operações Interna (DOI). The DOI had operatives from all the military sevices plus the police. The operatives in the DOI did not wear uniforms, financed their operations from a variety of official and unofficial sources, and, though nominally under the regional General Staff chain of command, in fact had a parallel chain of command to the Minister of the Army via CIE.

In the growing documentation about torture in Brazil, the most spectacular and extensive instances of this practice are directly linked to DOI networks. Much of the erosion of the hierarchy within the Brazilian military was also linked to the operational autonomy and the parallel chain of command built into the DOI-CIE system. At the height of the antisubversive struggle, a colonel in charge of a DOI, under the guise of the imperative of speed, efficiency, or secrecy, could bypass or *de facto* overrule the General Staff chain of command and work directly within the CIE.

The activities related to the DOI, always secret, virtually became clandestine and illegal, even by the military's own rules, by 1973–1975. Documented evidence that yields clear indicators of the emergence of a state within the state due to the loss of control over the security apparatus is just beginning to appear. For example, one analyst marshals data that indicate that during the height of the armed combat, in the 1968–1970 period, the guerrillas were responsible for forty-nine deaths, and the government for sixty. In the same period there were 216 formal, legal proceedings against guerrillas, and seven guerrillas "disappeared" after being captured. In 1974–1975, however, in the years when the guerrillas had been defeated militarily and the abertura had begun, the trial to "disappearance" ratio, instead of improving from the 30 to 1 ratio of 1968–1970, deteriorated dramatically—there were twenty-one legal proceedings, but twenty-five "disappearances."[15]

In my judgment, the explanation for this apparent anomaly of growing liberalization but increasing "disappearances" is that the repressive apparatus itself had acquired a significant degree of autonomy and was struggling as much against the abertura as it was against the armed combatants of the Left. One of the complex reasons for the paradoxical growth of strength of the SNI during the abertura was that most of the efforts to sabotage the abertura had links to the hard-liners who had fought in the DOI and who were thus operationally connected not to the SNI or to the professional soldiers in the General Staff as much as to the DOI and the CIE. The SNI, as dangerously powerful as it was, was seen by Ernesto Geisel and Golbery, in the early days of the abertura, as a potential instrument in their effort to impose their control over the army's relatively autonomous repressive apparatus.

From the beginning of the abertura in late 1973 until the end of the military government in 1985, the officers associated with the security community—whether in the navy, air force, military police, or the SNI—were predictably some of the strongest advocates of the argument that social conflicts posed threats to Brazil's internal security and national development and thus needed to be repressed. They had substantial power and no institutional stake

---

[15] These data and much of the above discussion of the DOI-CIE system are based upon an important and illuminating book in progress by Elio Gaspari, *Geisel e Golbery: O Sacerdote e o Feiticeiro*. For a table of organization of the chains of command and lines of communication between Brazil's many intelligence organizations, see Lagôa, *SNI*, anexo 7. For the role of the DOI and CIE in repression and torture, also see Kucinski, *Abertura: A História de uma Crise*, and Moreira Alves, *Estado e Oposição no Brasil (1964–1984)*. The most impeccably documented source on torture and "disappearances" is the publication of the archdiocese of São Paulo, *Brasil: Nunca Mais*, preface by Cardeal Paulo Evaristo Arns.

in changing the rules of the game in the direction of a political opening.

IN THE NEXT CHAPTER I will analyze why and how the Brazilian opening began in late 1973. However, the reader at all times must keep in mind that right up to the day Tancredo Neves, the civilian politician, was to take the presidential oath on March 15, 1985, there was always a hard-line tendency within the military—especially in the army—and this hard-line had their material and ideological base within the security community. The death while in army custody of the São Paulo journalist, Vladimir Herzog, that produced a crisis in 1975, the frustrated coup attempt by the Minister of the Army, General Sylvio Frota in 1977, the bombings of opposition newspaper stands and the Brazilian Bar Association in 1980, the extraordinary cover-up of the explosion that occurred outside a musical festival for youths in Riocentro in 1981, and the maneuvering to block the Electoral College from selecting Tancredo Neves for the presidency in 1985 were all linked to the security community and were all serious challenges to abertura. The Brazilian opening that its initiator, General Geisel, wanted to be ''a process of slow, gradual and secure decompression'' turned out to be an eleven-year, conflict-laden, intrastate, and societal struggle whose outcome was never certain.[16]

[16] Skidmore discusses all of these crises in ''Brazil's Slow Road to Democratization.'' Excellent detail on intramilitary conflicts can be found in Kucinski, *Abertura: A História de uma Crise*; and Stumpf and Pereira Filho, *A Segunda Guerra: Successão de Geisel*. According to Kucinski, the first time President Geisel explicitly and publicly used the phrase *distensão* was in a speech before government party leaders in Brasília in August 1974. See Kucinski, *Abertura: A História de uma Crise*, 41–42.

# CHAPTER THREE

# Abertura: Intrastate Conflicts and the Courtship of Civil Society

NO COMPLEX organization should be seen as a monolith. Conceptually, if we posit a highly repressive regime where the military is in control of the state apparatus, we can think of the military dimensions of the state as having a variety of *components*, and these components can, depending on their relative power and their actions, stand in various *configurations* to each other, even if we momentarily restrict artificially our analytic focus to only intramilitary politics within the state arena. Sociologically we could of course posit numerous components of the military regime and numerous configurations. For the purposes of this chapter, three components and four configurations are sufficient.

COMPONENT 1: *The Military as Government.* This refers to those military figures constituting the core leadership who direct the government of the polity. This is usually composed of a General President and his key staff, some of whom may be civilians.

COMPONENT 2: *The Security Community.* By this I mean those elements of the regime most directly involved in the planning and execution of repression, intelligence gathering, interrogation, torture, and internal clandestine armed operations.

COMPONENT 3: *The Military as Institution.* This includes the bulk of the military organization—those who staff the bases and carry out their routine training cycles, manage the complex network of the military-schooling system (except intelligence), do the day-to-day work of a military bureaucracy, and are available as a strategic reserve if there is a major national "emergency."[1]

---

[1] For a more discursive argument of the analytical and historical utility of the distinction between the "military as government" and the "military as institu-

Let us now posit four very different possible configurations within these components.

CONFIGURATION 1: *Apparent Fusion.* The three components could interact in a highly fused manner, and the outside observer could think that, prior internal differences notwithstanding, all components of the regime share a common threat perception and are acting in harmony.

CONFIGURATION 2: *Security Community Dominance.* We could imagine a situation where the security community becomes relatively autonomous, uses its power and autonomy to gain strategic influence within the military as institution, eventually captures the military as government, and then uses these augmented resources to control the military as institution.

CONFIGURATION 3: *Extrication Coup by Military as Institution.* It is possible to envisage a situation where powerful and strategically placed members of the military as institution come to the decision that the continuation of the military as government in office is extremely dangerous both to the unity and to other permanent interests of the military and stage an extrication coup to get the military out of office.

CONFIGURATION 4: *Liberalization Led by Military as Government.* There is also the possibility that the leaders of the military as government—alarmed that the security community might pursue a Configuration 2 goal, and convinced that this outcome is not in the permanent interest of the military as institution—might initiate a strategic course of action whereby they attempt to control the security community by regime liberalization, on the assumption that a regime of exception and repression privileges the power position of the security community. A major intramilitary factor in the success of this strategy is whether the military as government is able to gain control over more and more elements of the

tion," see my "Paths Toward Redemocratization: Theoretical and Comparative Considerations," esp. 72–78. I discuss the difficulties of institutionalizing military "organic-statist" regimes, in the last chapter of my *State and Society*, using the perspective of the predictable conflict between three distinct military components.

military as institution, or at least to remove them from the domain of the security community in the name of a normalization of professional activities.

Although I constructed these configurations abstractly, specialists on comparative civil-military relations in the modern world could readily match them with historical referents.[2] For example, in Greece in 1974 after the hard-line "military as government" created the Cyprus crisis and a near war with Turkey, the "military as institution" led by the Joint Chiefs of Staff assumed *de facto* institutional control and initiated the search for an extrication formula. The Chilean military, in the immediate aftermath of the overthrow of President Allende in 1973, approximated an "apparent fusion" configuration. Let us see how awareness of this "components and configurations" conceptual distinction helps us understand what could otherwise appear to be inexplicable or contradictory aspects of Brazilian military politics in the abertura.

HOW AND WHY did the Brazilian opening begin? In no sense was there sufficient external pressure on the military either from civil society or political society to force an abertura. There certainly was some opposition to the military rule in Brazil in late 1972. However, this opposition was much less serious than that faced by Pinochet in Chile in 1982–1984 or by Galtieri in Argentina in early 1982. In both Chile and Argentina, the "military as government" in fact launched major initiatives aimed at prolonging military rule and at narrowing the range of tolerated opposition.

Brazil saw no meaningful strike between 1969 and 1977. The entrepreneurs' campaign against statism in the economy did not really begin until late 1974. The effective protests of the Brazilian bar and press associations had yet to occur. The December 1973 year-end Gallup Poll showed that 65 percent of those polled in São Paulo (the eventual heart of civil society opposition) felt that 1974

[2] See Samuel P. Huntington, *Political Order in Changing Societies*, Chapter 4; Juan J. Linz, "Totalitarian and Authoritarian Regimes"; and my "Paths Toward Redemocratization."

would be a better year than 1973 had been, while only 14 percent felt it would be worse.[3] Nonetheless, the beginnings of distensão in Brazil are traceable to overtures to civil society in late 1973 and early 1974 by President-select General Ernesto Geisel and his key political advisor, General Golbery do Couto e Silva. Why did they, though faced with less opposition than their Chilean or Argentine opposite numbers, nevertheless initiate a liberalization process?

Golbery, in a series of five interviews with the author (in 1974, 1981, and 1982) about the abertura, argued that the original goals of the 1964 military coup were democratic in their long-run intentions. He also stated, in December 1974, that he thought that Linz's argument in *Authoritarian Brazil* was correct, namely that there was no long-term authoritarian solution available to Brazil that would have legitimacy. Finally, he put great stress on the deleterious effects of the 1969–1972 antiguerrilla campaign, which had led to a growing autonomy of the security community both within the state and especially within the military establishment itself. This growing autonomy, with its attendant ideological radicalization, was in Golbery's judgment both unnecessary and dangerous in late 1973: unnecessary because all credible armed opponents had been destroyed, and dangerous because the autonomy and radicalization of the security forces—if unchecked—would present a double threat to the Brazilian military. One threat was the danger of fragmentation and "Argentinianization," or worse its "Central Americanization." The other was of the growing separation of the fundamentally moderate forces of Brazilian society from the Brazilian military if the security community remained dominant.[4]

[3] Data obtained from the headquarters of Gallup Poll, Brazil, in São Paulo.

[4] My first interview with Golbery about the reasons for the abertura was on December 9, 1974, in Brasília. The last four interviews, also in Brasília, were conducted on September 15, 1981; May 20, 1982; June 16, 1982; and July 16, 1982. The fundamental sources on Golbery during the abertura are his July 1980 speech before the Escola Superior de Guerra, reproduced in his book, *Conjuntura Política Nacional: O Poder Executivo e Geopolítica do Brasil*, 2–37; and the *Veja* cover

To understand the balance of forces that Geisel and Golbery faced when they began their abertura, it is important to note that there is no evidence to suggest that Ernesto Geisel was chosen with an abertura mandate. No documented study of the selection process exists. However, it would appear safe to assert that no one could have been selected against the will of the outgoing president, General Médici, and without the support of the Minister of the Army, Orlando Geisel, who was the leader of the army—and the CIE-DOI system— during the height of the repression. Army four-star generals and some key SNI officials were also consulted in the selection process. By definition many of the above had played an active role in the 1968–1972 repression. If Orlando Geisel had campaigned for the presidency, he probably would have been selected. However, Orlando Geisel threw his support to his brother, Ernesto Geisel.

Ernesto Geisel had graduated at the top of his class at the three most important army schools. He had political experience dating from the 1930s, nationalistic credentials as a longtime supporter of the state oil company, PETROBRAS, and managerial credentials as the president of PETROBRAS. Along with Golbery, Ernesto Geisel, as Castello Branco's chief of the military household, had been an ally of the first president of the military regime in his losing struggle against the hard-line. However, Golbery asserts that a number of generals who supported Ernesto Geisel for the presidency did so only with the implicit understanding that he, Golbery, would not play a major role in the Geisel administration. In sum, the top hierarchy of the "military as institution" chose Ernesto Geisel to head the "military as government" because he had a number of valuable attributes; in the words of General Reynaldo de Mello, "he was the General who best combined political experience, economic experience and great prestige within the army."[5] No evidence exists, however, to support the case that he

---

stories on his resignation (August 12, 1981), 20–33, and the revelation of papers from his archives after his death (September 23, 1987), 20–31.

[5] My sources for this include General Reynaldo Mello de Almeida (ret.), who was chosen by Geisel to lead the politically crucial First Army of Rio from April 5, 1974, to December 2, 1976. He said Ernesto Geisel's name was put forward by

was chosen with an understanding that he should lead what came to be known as abertura.

HOW DID Ernesto Geisel see the intramilitary and interstate balance of forces in 1973? After I had completed most of my research for this book, General Geisel consented to give a rare interview. Concerning how he personally saw the situation he faced and the strategic course of action he devised, he was in implicit agreement with the Golbery interviews I have cited. However, five distinctive and telling themes emerged in the interview.

First, in Geisel's judgment, not only did he not have a mandate for distensão but significant military opinion (*"uma parte expressiva da opinião militar"*) opposed distensão. The opposition was strongest in those parts of the armed forces linked to the security apparatus, especially those involved actively in the counterguerrilla campaign.

Second, despite this opposition he was convinced that the country could not continue as it was, though he was also convinced that it would take a long time to change. He stressed that President Castello Branco had tried an abertura and that it had ended in the succession of the hard-line president, Costa e Silva, and in the extremely authoritarian Institutional Act Number 5: "I did not want to end with the same result."

Third, he emphasized repeatedly that it was necessary for him to lead and command the armed forces as hierarchical institutions: "I sought to lead as a Chefe." His role as "Chefe" was mentioned throughout the interview. He underscored that when he fired the Second Army commander during a crisis, he personally selected his successor. He acknowledged that this created a "negative reaction in the armed forces" but it helped him make his

---

his brother Orlando Geisel and seconded by the chief of the Military Cabinet, General Figueiredo (interview in Brasília, September 10, 1981). In another interview, General Carlos de Meira Mattos (ret.), stressed "the selection of Geisel was not done with a clear sense of abertura" (Rio de Janeiro, July 1982). Golbery explicitly said, "Orlando played the first role in choosing Ernesto. Figueiredo played the second most important role as a link between President Médici and Orlando" (interview, June 16, 1982).

point that he "would not accept that type of behavior." His conception of "Chefe" was complex. He imposed his authority, part of which derived from being a powerful general. But at the same time, a central part of his political project was to instill increasing respect for the office of the president, one of whose critical functions was that of being the Supreme Commander of the armed forces.

Fourth, in answer to my question as to what his timetable had been, he stopped me short and emphatically insisted that "I had no fixed timetable in my mind." He later added that he always intended to abolish Institutional Act Number 5 before finishing his fixed term as president.

Fifth, when I tried to explore his long-range goals when he launched distensão, he gave one of his infrequent smiles as if the inquiry itself was disingenuous. He asked me, "What is the first principle of Machiavelli? That governments should strive to keep power. I personally did not want to keep power forever but no government tells its allies that it wants to give power to the opposition." He concluded by saying that he knew he "would not advance without some retreats" but that throughout the entire abertura he was concerned with avoiding advances that would lead to irreversible retreats.[6]

The interview strengthens my previous impression that Geisel and Golbery were both crucial to the distensão but that given the balance of military forces they faced, and the longstanding distrust of Golbery within military circles, Golbery (who never in any interview referred to himself as a Chefe) needed Geisel as a precondition for Golbery to be "Golbery, the magician of the abertura." Geisel's assessment of the balance of power he faced also puts into perspective why the newly designated "military as government" began to reach out for allies in civil society.

Despite my interviews with Geisel and Golbery I am still not certain as to what their vision of an ideal Brazilian polity would be. To be sure, both had authoritarian tendencies and neither one said he wanted a democracy without any restrictions. However, at

---

[6] Interview with General Ernesto Geisel in Rio de Janeiro, July 17, 1985.

the very least, from a comparative perspective, they would seem to me to have something in common with the politically astute conservatives in England in 1832 and the Franco officials in Spain in the mid-1970s who tried to retain and stabilize their power by reconstituting its foundations. Part of this reconstitution was to make the military and the intelligence apparatus hierarchical institutions, and part was to reach out to civil society. A complex dialectic of regime concession and societal conquest thus began.

For Geisel the first step in reconstituting power involved loosening press censorship: "Censors are inept." He stressed that the existence of censorship allowed extremists to make unanswered charges even against the government.

In Golbery's judgment the security community thrived in an atmosphere of darkness and secrecy. Abuses were unrecorded, excesses unchecked. To counter such behavior in the security community, he felt the first important step would be to begin gradually to liberalize the press. To this end he spent a significant amount of time before and after Geisel's inauguration in direct high-level communications with key journalists and editors, trying to persuade them of the goals of the abertura project, while also sensitizing them to the constraints he and Geisel faced due to hard-line opposition.[7] Among those publications that gave important support to the liberalization project were the Rio daily *Jornal do Brasil* (the most influential political newspaper in Rio and Brasília); *Veja*, the first weekly in Brazil to reach a truly national audience; *Istoé*, a weekly with prestige and a faithful readership among the leaders of civil society in São Paulo; and *O Estado de S. Paulo,* which, though conservative, was a bastion for the defense of civil liberties, the rule of law, and freedom of the press.

Another element of civil society that was a high priority for Golbery and Geisel was the church. They were worried by grow-

[7] He emphasized this in his December 9, 1974, interview when the press was still censored, and again on June 16, 1982. See the insightful article by Celina Rabello Duarte. It correctly calls attention both to the courting of the press by Geisel and Golbery as an arm against the military, and to the means the government still retained to keep the press within desired parameters, "Imprensa e Redemocratização no Brasil."

ing church criticism of the regime. The period between Geisel's final selection as president by the electoral college on January 15 and his inauguration on March 15, 1974, was one of active bridge-building. Although the event was not reported in the press until February 28, the Secretary General of the National Confederation of Brazilian Bishops (CNBB) met with Geisel's transition team on January 15.[8] Golbery during the abertura met on a number of occasions in São Paulo, and at least once at Golbery's rural retreat outside of Brasília, with the most institutionally powerful church leader, Cardinal Arns of São Paulo. According to Golbery, the two chief concerns of the church at this time were torture and disappearances, and these were two issues where Geisel and Golbery—and the church hierarchy—faced common opponents. As Golbery recalled the period, "five cardinals were at Geisel's inauguration and this was the result of the work of the three prior months."[9] Geisel, in the interview, asserted that though Golbery talked to the CNBB before his inauguration he, as a non-Catholic, did not, but he said that he developed good relations with the papal nuncio, with whom he talked more than ten times while president, and that the pope did not once attack his government.

One of the clearest illustrations of the conscious use by Geisel of civil society against military extremists was his action following the death—within a day of being placed in an interrogation unit of the Second Army in São Paulo—of Vladimir Herzog, a journalist who had been working on an educational television show. Herzog's death sparked an extraordinary civic reaction culminating in an emotional ecumenical service in the cathedral, with the participation of Cardinal Arns, a reaction that is correctly treated as a historic protest of civil society against the state. In Brasília there was a debate as to whether President Geisel should or should not go to São Paulo after the local military, and São Paulo government officials had failed to block the protest. He chose to go. On a number of occasions during his São Paulo visit he broke protocol to mix with civic groups. Twenty-three presi-

[8] *O Estado de S. Paulo*, February 28, 1974.
[9] Interview with General Golbery, June 16, 1982.

dents of São Paulo workers federations were called to a meeting on short notice. They were surprised to see President Geisel enter. Geisel engaged in a rare, hour-long question-and-answer period, at the end of which he announced the creation of a new university scholarship program for the children of union members.[10] Geisel's political ally in São Paulo, Governor Paulo Egydio, whose authority, and thus Geisel's, had been challenged by the Second Army extremists, hosted a reception for Geisel where Geisel met prominent advocates for a rule of law. Interviews and a reading of his activities that day in São Paulo leave the clear impression that he consciously made an effort to get closer to civil society and to use an aroused civil society against military extremists. At the airport, Geisel made a point of hugging only one person, the surprised José Mindlin, the Secretary of Culture for the state of São Paulo, who had defended Herzog against attacks by the security community.[11] The clamor of civil society allowed Geisel to say to army comrades that he would never tolerate such a death in a military facility again. Months later, when another such death occurred, Geisel immediately sacked the commanding general of the Second Army, and in the aftermath, General Confucio Danton de Paula Avelino, the chief of the CIE and a central figure in the resistance to abertura within hard-line army intelligence circles, was removed.[12] In the opinion of Golbery, the reaction of civil society—and Geisel's ability to associate himself eventually with it— immensely strengthened the government's hand against their most dangerous opponents within the security apparatus.[13] The episode also of course made civil society in São Paulo more powerful and is, like the opposition's stunning victories in the 1974 elections, but one of many examples of the complex dialectic in the Brazilian abertura between regime concession and societal conquest.

Let me conclude this section by returning to the discussion of military *components* and *configurations* but relaxing our original

[10] The entire back page of the *O Estado de S. Paulo* of October 31, 1975, is devoted to the details of Geisel's activities on October 30 in São Paulo.

[11] Interview with José Mindlin, São Paulo, May 25, 1982.

[12] Robello Duarte, "Impresa e Redemocratização no Brasil," 191–192.

[13] Interview with General Golbery, Brasília, June 16, 1982.

assumption that we have to restrict our analysis to intramilitary politics and reintroducing political and civil society. The military as government, military as institution, and the security community acted in apparent fusion from 1969 to 1973. I say apparent because the soft-line Castellistas were virtually silenced, but still present. In fact, Castellistas (followers of former President Castello Branco) such as Geisel and Golbery worried that Brazil was on the brink of security community dominance. They felt such dominance would eventually cause great divisions both within the military as institution and within the country at large, and thus dash their own vision of Brazil as a major Western power.[14] President-select Geisel and General Golbery thus attempted to use their power base in the military as government to lead the military as institution on a course of liberalization. The empowerment of parts of civil society (especially the press) and parts of political society was crucial to the design. This much is fairly clear. Memoirs need to be published, archives opened, interviews granted and systematic research done, but even at this early date the components and configurations framework may partially resolve some of the abertura's more puzzling paradoxes.

PARADOX 1: Why, if the incoming "military as government" began to plan the distensão in September 1973, did more than two-thirds of all "disappearances" of political prisoners between 1964 and 1979 happen in 1973–1974?[15]

[14] This vision has been a key element of Castellista thought for over thirty years. They associated being a Western modern power with some form of democracy because all of the post-World War II Western powers were. Part of this vision had its origin in Brazil's participation in World War II in Italy. See my *The Military in Politics*, 239–244.

[15] The office of the diocese of the archbishop of São Paulo made a major effort to document the "disappearance" of political prisoners after they were captured by military organizations. For the entire 1964–1979 period, at least 77 of the 125 recorded disappearances occurred in 1973 and 1974. See *Brasil: Nunca Mais*, Anexo III. The archdiocese's report notes: "The early months of the Geisel administration were a period in which the forces of repression opted for a method of concealing cases of imprisonment followed by death, in order to avoid the decreasing credibility of repeated reports of people 'being run over,' 'committing suicide,' and 'attempting to escape' in the climate of greater press freedom. As a result, cases

EXPLANATION: The extremists in the security community, fearing they would lose their autonomy, waged a new round of warfare against leftist organizations, both to eliminate them,and to convince the "military as institution" that the subversive' threat was real and that distensão was a dangerous mistake.[16]

PARADOX 2: Why, if the incoming military as government feared the growing autonomy of the security community, did they use and even strengthen the SNI?

EXPLANATION: Early in his administration President Geisel gave the head of the SNI a stake in the military as government's abertura project by making him his heir-apparent.[17] He then tried to use the resources of the SNI to gain control over the army, especially over the hard-liners whose base of strength and resistance was the CIE-DOI network.[18]

---

of 'disappearance' became common. . . . Security organizations seemed to have aimed at a clean sweep of all groups on the Left, an annihilation of everything that had resisted previous repression'' (*Brasil: Nunca Mais*, 64). Kucinski, in his *Abertura: A História de uma Crise*, 44–46, has a chart of people who "disappeared" after the security community knew of the selection of Geisel and a vivid account of the heightened pace of security community repressive activity.

[16] This was stressed in my 1981 and 1982 interviews with General Golbery and in my interviews with General Reynaldo Mello de Almeida, who was made the commander of the First Army after the inauguration of President Geisel. Also see Kucinski, *Abertura: A História de uma Crise*.

[17] Stumpf and Pereira Filho's entire book, *A Segunda Guerra: Sucessão de Geisel*, revolves around the argument that Geisel and Golbery felt they lost the "first war" in 1965, when Geisel (as chief of President Castello Branco's military household) and Golbery (as the head of the SNI) were defeated by the hard-line, and had to accept the imposition of a hard-line candidate, General Costa e Silva, as the next president. According to Stumpf and Pereira Filho, Geisel made the strategic decision in 1973 that liberalization would be ensured only if he could control who his successor would be. Their book argues that during a meeting with his key advisers in late 1973 Geisel stressed this point and instructed that, although he did not rule out a civilian successor, his probable successor would be General João Baptista Figueiredo. The battle of Geisel to control his succession thus became "The Second War" (see pp. 15–24). Golbery, in interviews, confirmed the bitter experience of 1965, but did not give details on Geisel's selection process of Figueiredo.

For another account of Geisel's style and the selection process, see Getúlio Bittencourt, *A Quinta Estrela: Como se Tenta Fazer um Presidente no Brasil*.

[18] This general picture—with some variations, to be sure—was related to me by

PARADOX 3: If the new "military as government" had a distensão agenda, why were "hard-liners" appointed to many key positions in the military as institution, why did President Geisel never speak out openly against the torture of the 1969–1973 period, and why did the most dangerous challenge emerge from within the military as government itself—the near-coup attempt by Geisel's hand-selected Minister of the Army?

EXPLANATION: President Geisel took over the military when hard-liners still had great power within the military as institution. One way to keep them from mobilizing against his agenda was to not violate hierarchy in purely military appointments, and even to give the hard-line some initial representation in the military as government while he slowly changed the balance of forces within all three arenas of the polity. On a personal level, Ernesto Geisel was silent about the torture of 1969–1973 because his brother, Orlando, who helped make him president, had been Minister of the Army during that period and in charge of the CIE-DOI system. The question of the near coup attempt by Minister of the Army General Frota is more complicated. He became hard-line only *after* he joined the government.[19] A plausible theoretical explanation is that strong constituencies tempt aspirant leaders to be the voice of that constituency. General Frota wanted to be president. The chief of the SNI was already the candidate of the military as government. Frota attempted to be the voice—and thus the candidate—of the hard-line constituency associated with the CIE and the security community.

PARADOX 4: If Geisel was the author of distensão, why is he also known as the "dictator of the abertura?"

EXPLANATION: By temperament and governing style he was a

two of Brazil's most knowledgeable journalists, Golbery, and two generals who held key commands during this period.

[19] Stumpf and Pereira Filho, in *A Segunda Guerra*, in fact argue that General Frota, while commandant of the First Army during the Médici government, helped fight against torture in his command (see p. 23). Kucinski, in his *Abertura*, goes further and says Frota made surprise visits to interrogation centers suspected of torture in his command. The most infamous prison was relocated to a secret location in order to avoid Frota's control (see p. 67).

"monarchical centralist" and extremely authoritarian, but it was against the military as institution—especially the High Command—that he attempted to exercise dictatorial power.[20] His major goal was to remove the military from routine involvement in national politics. For the first time in the history of the military regime, the president, without prior consultation with the high command or even his Minister of the Army, single-handedly and summarily removed a hard-line officer from his post (General Ednardo, who was the commander of the Second Army in São Paulo during the Herzog crisis).[21] Most importantly, he selected his own presidential successor without conferring with the high command. His "dictatorship" over the military was also partly a function of the fact that his key political ally, General Golbery, was distrusted by the military and focused mainly on the arenas of civil and political society. President Geisel's retention and periodic use of powerful authoritarian instruments, such as Institutional Act Number 5, against political and civil society were a function of his authoritarian temperament as well as a way of assuring the security community and the military as institution that the military as government was in command and would not lose control of the liberalization process.

PARADOX 5: If distensão as a project started in late 1973, why were there more hard-liners in Figueiredo's high command of 1980 than there had been in Geisel's in 1977, and why did the SNI seem to be growing in relative power?[22]

[20] When President Costa e Silva became incapacitated, the army High Command met and selected his successor, and retained great presumptive power over major political decisions. Geisel was determined to act as full commander in chief and to reduce the High Command's power.

[21] Stumpf and Pereira Filho, *A Segunda Guerra*, 113. According to this account, Ernesto Geisel did consult his brother Orlando Geisel, who said, "Demita, com humilhação" ("Sack, with humiliation"). Whether this particular account is accurate or not, the style of Geisel's dismissal of General Ednardo was virtually without precedent in Brazilian military history. Geisel's chief of the Military Cabinet at that time, General Hugo Abreu, in his memoirs, *O Outro Lado do Poder*, said the style of the dismissal offended many military commanders, especially those in the security community (see pp. 111–114).

[22] Kucinski's *Abertura* presents a table where he classifies (by name and post)

EXPLANATION: Part of the explanation appears to be that the colonels and brigadier generals most personally involved in the intense years of repression (1969–1973) were radicalized by the experience, had the most to fear if the security community lost control of the process, and were now three- and four-star generals in the military as institution. Also, President Figueiredo, unlike his predecessor President Geisel, was not by temperament or presidential style a "dictator," or even a strong leader, over the military or the SNI. Finally, since President Figueiredo did not effectively control the presidential succession process, the director of the SNI (and his core staff) could best increase their own chances of controlling the next presidency if the security community regularly supplied (or made?) evidence of dangerous conflicts and subversive trends in the Brazilian polity.

---

all thirteen members of the army High Command in 1977 and 1980 according to three categories: "Liberal Castellistas," "Hard Castellistas," and "Hard Line" (p. 72). He classifies two of the thirteen members of the December 1977 High Command as "Hard-Line." He classifies ten of the thirteen members of the June 1980 High Command as "Hard-Line." The major Brazilian newspapers all have specialists who are full-time military-watchers. In 1981 I asked one of these journalists (whose own politics were rather conservative) to draw me a simple chart of the changing attitudes of the High Command over time. He arrived at the conclusion that the 1981 High Command was, by Brazilian standards, very hard-line. Also see Stepan, "O Que Estão Pensando os Militares."

CHAPTER 4

# Military Discourse and Abertura

STRATEGIES of retention and reconstruction of power involve changing, but controlling, the terms of the discourse. For Michel Foucault, discourse involves technologies of power and practice and is thus in need of constant reproduction. For an understanding of processes of transition, tasks of opposition, and the continuing problems of democratic consolidation, military discourse merits much closer critical inquiry than it has received to date.[1]

In the Brazilian case, the abertura entailed a dialectic between regime concession and societal conquest in which the architects of the initial opening attempted to define the content, and delimit the boundaries, of liberalization. It is vital to focus on the dialectic of regime concession and societal conquest for two reasons. First, if the major impetus for change remains regime concession, what is given might be taken away. Second, the boundaries of what is given might be liberalization but not democratization. In this chapter I will examine how the content of national security doctrine changed and did not change during the abertura. If there had

[1] For Michel Foucault, see "Truth and Power" and "Power and Strategies." Also on the control and appropriation of discourse, see Pierre Bourdieu, *Ce que parler veut dire*. For numerous examples of "ideological operation" in an authoritarian setting and the forms of critical "counterdiscourses," see Marilena Chauí, *Cultura e Democracia: O Discurso Competente e Outras Falas*. For the task of reconstructing the discourse in order to facilitate democratic consolidation, see Oscar Landi, *El discurso sobre lo posible (La democracia y el realismo político)*. For telling analyses of Latin American military discourse, see Hernan Vidal, "The Politics of the Body: The Chilean Junta and the Anti-Fascist Struggle"; Eurico de Lima Figueredo, *Os Militares e a Democracia*; Giselle Munizaga, *El discurso público de Pinochet: Un análisis semiológico*; Carina Perelli, *Convencer o someter: El discurso militar*; and her "Amnistía sí, amnistía no, amnistía puede ser . . . : La constitución histórica de un tema político en el Uruguay de la postransición," and the previously cited work by Genaro Arriagada, *El Pensamiento Político de los Militares*.

been no dialectic between concession and conquest, what type of democracy did the theorists of national-security doctrine envisage? I will begin with an analysis of the formal doctrinal documents of the Escola Superior de Guerra (Superior War College. I do so not because the ESG was itself a center of political or doctrinal initiative in the abertura. The period of greatest doctrinal initiative was in 1952–1956, when many of its key ideas were shaped. The period of greatest political importance was between 1964 and 1967, when many of the 1952–1956 core group formulated and implemented the policies of the first military government.[2]

From the perspective of organization theory, no organization—least of all a military organization—wants to coexist with an alternative claimant to doctrinal and political authority in its sphere of action. For this reason, the Superior War College, despite its continued fame, lost much of its power as an independent institution after the military coup of 1964. This power loss was compounded by a number of other factors. By the early 1970s, the military ministries had moved almost entirely to the new capital in Brasília while the Superior War College remained in Rio de Janeiro and became geographically marginalized from the center of military power. In addition, the commandant of the ESG, normally a four-star officer, could not be a member of the Higher Military Command which was a major power broker in the military government. Finally, colonels could only stay on the permanent staff of the school for two years and the staff did not really have any full-time researchers. A number of the brightest stars of the graduating class turned down offers to join the permanent staff because the "fastest track" was in Brasília. In separate interviews both the acting commandant of the ESG and General Golbery acknowledged that the ESG played an extremely small independent policy role throughout the abertura.[3] Specifically, no ESG studies were

[2] In my *The Military in Politics* I discuss the formative period of the Escola Superior de Guerra in Chapter 8, and its impact on the policy of the first military government in Chapters 10–11.

[3] Interviews with the acting commandant of the ESG, August 1981, and with General Golbery, July 16, 1982. The best general discussion of the decline of the

forwarded directly to any ministries, but were only forwarded to the General Staff of the Armed Forces (EMFA), a relatively small and uninfluential body.

Notwithstanding all this, the ESG performed a central function within the Brazilian military. Precisely because the Brazilian military valued doctrinal order and subjected its members to a systematic socialization process at all levels of its schooling system, they had a requirement for one institution constantly to systematize, update, and disseminate the official doctrine of national security and development. The ESG had this task. Thus, although not a center of initiative, it was the authorized source of military ideology for the military as institution. It therefore becomes extremely important to study the evolution of ESG doctrine during the abertura because the entire military schooling and socialization network, state agencies such as the SNI, and the military-dominated legal system that produced the National Security Laws used as their doctrinal base the official documents of the ESG.

It is also important to study because the ideological work and reach of the ESG among civilians was intense throughout the abertura. For example, the 1982 annual report of the school noted that in addition to the regular full-time courses in the school (of which civilians normally constituted at least half of the students), the school offered a special seventy-hour extension course for 150 aspiring civilian leaders at its headquarters three times a year. The Alumni Association (ADESG), with the help of the school, also gave a sixteen-week extension course in twenty-one cities. In 1963, only 361 students attended these extension courses; by 1976, attendance had increased tenfold. By 1982, ADESG had also printed 189 issues of their glossy publication, *Segurança e Desenvolvimento*, which that year had a printing of 15,000 copies.[4]

Having established that the ESG maintained an active ideological civil-military campaign during the abertura, we must examine

Escola Superior de Guerra is found in the previously cited dissertation by Alexandre de Souza Costa Barros, "The Brazilian Military," esp. 168–191.

[4] The above is based upon visits to the ADESG headquarters in São Paulo, an interview with the commandant of the ESG, General Alzir Benjamin Chaloub, and a speech by General Chaloub, "A Escola Superior de Guerra."

the content of this campaign. My principal sources were: (1) The periodically modified basic book (*Manual Básico*) of official doctrine, normally running some 350 pages; (2) a special book issued in 1981 (*Complementos da Doutrina*) that gave a somewhat more discursive and tentative treatment of doctrinal evolution; (3) the hour-by-hour lesson plan of the school from 1974 to 1983; (4) the names and topics of outside speakers to the school for 1974–1983; (5) the end-of-course collective exercise written by the graduating students, in which they recommend solutions to policy problems; and (6) interviews with civilian and military faculty members.[5]

These sources revealed developments worth assessing. From as early as 1966 democracy and Marxism-Leninism were depicted in ESG doctrine as the fundmental modern antagonism.[6] This framing of the conflict had implications. From the late 1960s, ESG theorists stressed that the one-party system was a core characteristic of Marxism-Leninism, and that all democratic systems must have more than one party. Thus, from the beginning of the military regime there was legitimate space for nongovernment parties in the ESG canon; indeed, they were an ideological necessity. For these doctrinal reasons (as well as for powerful reasons of history), the Mexican one-party system was never considered a desired option for Brazil. The doctrinal status of the ''opposition'' (implicit in the vision of the necessity of more than just a government party) evolved slowly. In 1975, 1977–1978, and 1979, in the book of official doctrine under the heading of *deconformismo*, opposition was recognized as a legitimate expression of dissenting opinion about government policy, but little was said. In 1981, however, the legitimacy of the opposition was given explicit emphasis in the *Complementos da Doutrina*: ''The recognition of the right of political opposition is one of the fundamentals of democracy. . . . The principle of liberty assures to everyone the right of

[5] All of the written sources were consulted at the library of the school in Rio de Janeiro, which is open to scholars. In 1979 the book of official doctrine was called *Doutrina Básica*, and in 1981 it was *Complementos da Doutrina*. A senior civilian faculty member has written a historical survey of the school doctrine that was published in commercial form: Antonio de Arruda, *ESG: História de Sua Doutrina*.

[6] Arruda, *ESG: História de Sua Doutrina*, 229.

disagreeing with those who, at the moment, hold political power."[7] Another major change of emphasis in the 1981 *Complementos da Doutrina* was the status of "participation," which was given only a few lines in 1975, 1977–1978, and 1979. In 1981, however, there was the acknowledgment that the spirit of participation "has recently gained ground in the national consciousness" and an entire chapter was devoted to the topic. An effort was made to show how participation, as grounded in papal thinking, was, if properly understood, an integral part of ESG doctrine.[8] In fact, in 1980–1981 informal discussion about participation was serious enough within the school that the *Complementos da Doutrina* said that, though participation was important, the traditional binomial motto of the school's doctrine, "Security—Development," did not really need to become a tripé (tripod) of "Security—Development—Participation" because it was already incorporated into ESG thinking.[9] Further, the pre-election year of 1981 featured the most extensive doctrinal treatment yet of the status of elections within democracy. The *Complementos* said that "a political system can only be democratic if it emanates from the people," from the "free choice of the people's representatives." Thus "democracy presupposes representativeness obtained by means of electoral competitiveness."[10]

Finally, for their collective graduation exercise, the members of the 1981 class were divided into twelve working groups, and each one was asked to address the question of "How to perfect democracy in Brazil?" Almost all of them criticized the excessive centralization of government, spoke of the necessity of a more autonomous judiciary, of the importance of a better distribution of income, greater public participation, and a stronger domestic industry.

The changes in ESG doctrine from 1974 to 1981 had allowed them to incorporate four of the key political concepts of critical

---

[7] Estado-Maior das Forças Armadas, Escola Superior de Guerra, *Complementos da Doutrina*, 94.

[8] Ibid., Chapter 6.

[9] Ibid., 107.

[10] Ibid., quotes from pp. 91 and 100.

groups in civil society—opposition, participation, nongovernmental parties, and elections—into the national-security discourse. A lively debate between linguists and social scientists who are engaged in discourse analysis centers on how groups with power attempt to appropriate meaning, that is, to utilize for their own purposes powerful symbols that emerged originally as a vehicle for criticism. In the most extreme cases this involves "resemanticization."[11] A closer textual analysis of the ESG discourse allows us not only to see how national security theorists had appropriated much of the critical vocabulary of civil society in the abertura but also to locate this vocabulary within a larger ESG canon so that the latent critical power of the vocabulary was neutralized.

Let us examine ESG techniques of neutralization more closely. We have seen how in 1966 democracy was formally stated as the major modern antagonist of Marxism-Leninism. By 1969, however, the school formally elaborated the "principle of self-defense" of democracy.[12] Throughout the abertura this principle was interpreted to mean that the president could exact, and the military court system could enforce, far-reaching and stringent security measures. For example, a constitutional amendment of 1978 explicitly gave the president the right to declare a state of siege for up to 120 days without congressional approval.[13] Also, the softened National Security Law of 1978 still gave the military justice system "the exclusive competence" to adjudicate a broad range of offenses against national security.[14] Both of these powerful prerogatives were explicitly defended as logical outgrowths of the principle of democratic self-defense.

We have also seen the importance given to opposition. However, virtually every discussion of opposition, which was seen as a legitimate expression of dissenting opinion about government policy, was counterbalanced by a discussion of "contestation."

[11] For numerous examples of efforts to "capture the discourse" and "appropriate meaning," see the references cited in note 1.

[12] Arruda, *ESG: História de Sua Doutrina*, 230.

[13] Constitutional Amendment Number 11, October 13, 1978, Articles 155–158.

[14] Lei de Segurança Nacional, Lei No. 6.620, December 17, 1978, Article 52.

Contestation was seen as a systematic attack on the regime itself and thus illegitimate and subject to state repressive measures deriving from the principle of self-defense.[15] The definition of what was opposition and what was contestation—especially in the liberalizing but still authoritarian context of Brazil's abertura—was implicitly left to the state.

Finally, what did the ESG perceive as elections? Their definition of what constituted acceptable elections in a democracy was permissively vague. "Democracy is a political system which cannot exist without a plurality of parties. The process for the investiture of the representatives of the people is what can vary—direct or indirect elections, universal or limited suffrage, obligatory or voluntary voting—but what can never be allowed is an exclusive party, a one party system."[16]

Let us now return to the 1981 year-end graduation-class exercise about how to perfect Brazilian democracy. As anthropologists, linguists, and political scientists well know, it is not enough simply to examine texts. Power manifests itself in nonissues. It is critically important to examine silences. Not one essay advocated abrogation of the National Security Law or of the president's right to declare a state of siege. Eleven of the twelve were silent about the central question of direct elections for the presidency. One did, however, recommend direct presidential elections.

When one examines the guest speakers at the school one notes other silences: the lack of involvement of virtually any of the new civilian leaders of civil and political society. In 1979 two opposition senators, Franco Montoro and Paulo Brossard, spoke at the school. In 1980 one of the key entrepreneurs in favor of abertura, Paulo Villares, spoke at the school. However, in 1980, 1981, and 1982 not one opposition senator, not one official representative of the Confederation of Brazilian Bishops, not one trade-union leader, and not one leading social scientist in any way associated with the democratic opposition spoke.

[15] See Arruda, *ESG: História de Sua Doutrina*, 58–63, for a historical discussion of the "opposition" versus "contestation" distinction in ESG doctrine.

[16] *Complementos da Doutrina*, 92.

What should we conclude from this analysis? The most obvious point is that the ESG (and thus the officially sanctioned doctrine within the entire school system of the "military as institution") lagged behind the "military as government" of Geisel and Golbery, and even more behind the country at large. In 1981, a soon-to-be-retired army general, who strongly supported the abertura, remarked bitterly that the military ideological campaigns of 1961–1964 and 1968–1972 "had required an intense educational effort. Thus any effort at a real abertura to democracy will require an immense resocialization in the ESG and all the service schools. Nothing serious of this sort has started yet. We have lost seven years of abertura."[17]

A less obvious point is that despite the deafening silence about direct elections, the equivocation about "opposition" versus "contestation," and the advocacy of liberalization but not democratization, this modified doctrine of the military as institution probably narrowed the alternatives available to the hard-liners in the security community. The effort to capture the discourse is not without costs and consequences. Given that the modified doctrine insisted upon some form of participation, some form of opposition, some form of decentralization, and, most importantly, some form of elections (even if in an indirect electoral college), how supportive could the doctrine be to any possible efforts to mobilize a *de facto* coup aiming at stopping indirect elections, at founding a new hard-line regime, and, if necessary, at closing Congress? Let us make no mistake, however. The modified doctrine was fully consistent with the military as government's plan to manage the presidential succession in 1985 and thus not to let the opposition have a serious chance to assume the presidency until 1991.

In my interviews with active-duty military officers in the 1981–1982 period, the attitudes I detected in the written ESG documents were, by and large, echoed. For example, I had extensive interviews with two military judges on the Supreme Military Court who, due to their past actions before coming to the court, or their published opinions since coming to the court, made me think that

---

[17] Interview, not for direct citation, in 1981.

they would entertain some reservations about the National Security Law. Neither one did. Both argued that democracy needed safeguards and that the National Security Law was precisely the type of instrument needed for a "strong democracy" instead of a "liberal democracy." The key to a "strong democracy" was that it somehow institutionalized the *principle of self-defense.* One made a point of saying that, given the balance of forces within the military, the revised national security law of 1978 should be seen as a modest step forward for those favoring abertura but at the same time as a guarantee to those who were frightened that abertura might get out of hand. He said that if I understood this then I should understand why he considered the revised National Security Law "the first law of the abertura."[18] Both stressed, however, that by the end of the 1980s much of the National Security Law would either have been revised or have fallen into *de facto*, if not *de jure*, disuse. It is important for me to stress that, although only a distinct minority of the military officers I interviewed in 1981–1982 wanted a military president in 1985, virtually none of them thought that the opposition could or should gain the presidency in 1985. The overwhelming sentiment within the military was that the opposition could not realistically contemplate power until the

---

[18] In the last of my long interviews with General Golbery about the dynamics of the abertura, I raised the general question of the surprising continuity of national security doctrine in the ESG. His first response was that the ESG was not in fact very important as a center of ideology or policy after the military took power in 1964 and that he almost never used any of their policy analyses. I countered with an observation that nonetheless the ESG doctrine had significantly lagged behind the dynamics of the abertura and that as long as ESG doctrine remained unchanged, it persisted as the hierarchically legitimated discourse used to indoctrinate officers at all levels of military socialization. I added further that the very broad definition of security that was still accepted at the school enabled the SNI to claim that its very wide interpretation of its duties was consistent with ESG doctrine. Golbery acknowledged that this was probably so and then went on to say that his primary activities within the abertura had been oriented toward political parties and civil society and that he was only marginally involved in formulating strategy or tactics for the military. To my surprise, my overall judgment of our interviews is that the area of the Brazilian polity to which General Golbery had devoted the least of his formidable theoretical and political energies was the military.

proregime president selected via the upcoming electoral college finished his term in 1991.

If the military believed they could keep power until 1991, why in fact did they lose power to a united opposition in 1985? Why did the regime come to an end? These questions are addressed in the next chapter.

# CHAPTER 5

# The End of the Regime:
# Political Society and the Military

IN A STRUGGLE for democracy, the relationships of power in an authoritarian regime depend, on the one hand, on the regime's capacity to lead its allies and to maintain the unity of its coercive apparatus, and, on the other hand, on the capacity of the democratic opposition to constitute itself and to generate support for a ruling alternative. In 1970 the Brazilian regime had great capacity to lead its allies, the military approximated a "fusion configuration," and the opposition was small and divided. By 1982 the power relationship concerning regime allies and regime opposition had altered sharply in favor of the opposition. Despite this, the coercive apparatus, unlike Greece in 1974 and Argentina in 1982, was not in decomposition. Systematic examination of regime termination, therefore, requires both a general analysis of macro-socioeconomic forces and a specific analysis of the factors that alter the will and capacity of the coercive apparatus to maintain the regime. Elsewhere I have done a comparative analysis of authoritarian state power and the evolution of opposition strategies in the four bureaucratic-authoritarian regimes of Brazil, Argentina, Chile, and Uruguay.[1] Here I will be quite selective about macro-socioeconomic forces in order to examine in more detail the specific interaction between new capacities in civil and political society and their impact on military capacity and will.

## ALTERED RELATIONSHIPS OF POWER:
## ACHIEVEMENTS AND LIMITS, 1970 AND 1982

The relative power of the military regime had, after the election of 1982, declined significantly from its height of the Médici era in

---

[1] See my "State Power and the Strength of Civil Society in the Southern Cone of Latin America."

1970. One very important factor in the military's loss of civilian elite allies was the fact that the military had destroyed all credible enemies from the violent Left by 1972. Moreover, as Weffort makes clear, the overwhelming majority of the Left—quite unlike in Chile—had undergone a deep ideological reassessment and valorized democratic rules of the game to a much greater degree than ever before in Brazilian history.[2]

As Lamounier's data also demonstrate, the electoral game had shifted against the government, and more of the opposition were identified with electoral politics. In 1970 the government party won 48.4 percent of the vote in the lower federal house, the opposition only 21.3 percent, and the fact that null and blank votes at 30.3 percent outnumbered the opposition party vote shows the low status of the opposition party. In the 1982 elections to the same chamber, the government won only 36.7 percent of the votes. The nongovernment parties more than doubled their vote, to 48 percent, and null and blank votes were cut in half, to 15.1 percent.[3] At the level of elite politics, the entrepreneurs, first in their anti-estatização campaign of 1974–1976, and later in their annual *Gazeta Mercantil* poll, demonstrated a desire for greater routinized access to decision making and less state autonomy. In addition, many middle-class groups, such as lawyers and journalists, often joined forces with the new working-class movements in common cause against the authoritarian regime.[4] In theoretical terms, therefore, the military government in 1982 had lost its *raison d'être* in terms of credible threat, had a much narrower base of elite support (by 1982, the Gallup Poll indicated that more than 90 percent of the top socioeconomic group in São Paulo wanted direct elections for the presidency), and faced a larger, more autonomous, but democratic, opposition. The Brazilian military were no longer sailing with the economic winds, as in 1968–1972,

---

[2] See Francisco Weffort, "Why Democracy?"

[3] See Lamounier's discussion, in "Authoritarian Brazil Revisited," of the increasing plebiscitary character of elections and of the slow but cumulative growth of the legitimacy of the Brazilian Democratic Movement (MDB) as an authentic opposition party.

[4] See Stepan, ed., *Democratizing Brazil*.

but instead, by 1981–1982, against a gale of economic adversity. Worse, they appeared to have no clear strategy as to how to surmount the most severe economic crisis in the country's history.[5] Brazil's "Brumairean moment" had long passed. Few of the military's initial allies were still willing to abdicate the everyday management of their political affairs to the military.

Why then did the military think they could, and should, keep the opposition from power until 1991? What did they fear the most? What were the major resources they felt they could utilize to achieve their goals?

First, it is important to stress that although they did not altogether rule out the selection of a military president for the 1985–1991 term, most military men expressed a preference for a pro-government civilian who would maintain the regime. By and large they felt this would be the best way to protect the interests of the military as an institution. Why did they want a civilian? The acting commandant of the ESG summed up an opinion I heard many times. He argued— correctly—that the military percentage of the budget had declined in the last decade.

> We are losing technical capacity. We now have a great role in the international economy but we have no capacity to project our power outside of Brazil. Our equipment is very old. We have been restricting ourselves in weapons requests in order to get a good image as a government. It is hard to ask a military government for this support because we are the government. It will be easier for the military to advance our legitimate claims against a government led by a civilian.[6]

With only a slight change of emphasis, at least four other generals, without urging, made the same argument. I should also note that the military share of the budget had soared in Uruguay, Chile, and Argentina during their bureaucratic-authoritarian periods, and

---

[5] Ample evidence is found in Albert Fishlow, "A Tale of Two Presidents: The Political Economy of Crisis Management."

[6] Interview with Admiral José Maria do Amaral Oliveira, Rio de Janeiro, August 1981.

that the budgetary argument for extrication within the Southern Cone was uniquely Brazilian.[7]

A more diffuse but real anxiety within the military was their awareness of their declining prestige in the public's eyes. They were worried about charges of corruption and the inevitable loss of support attendant on two decades of rule. The military families most associated with the military as institution, but not directly connected with the perks or cares of the military as government, were provided with continuous accounts in Brazil's superb and liberalized press of the excesses of the security community and of corruption within the military government.[8] An indication of how widespread doubts about military capacity and honesty were (especially among the top socioeconomic groups) is revealed in Gal-

[7] I will elaborate on the question of military budgets and arms in Chapter 6.

[8] The 1981 Riocentro incident demoralized much of the rank and file of the military as institution because even though hundreds of youthful bystanders could have been killed, no serious inquiries were made. The security community was clearly involved, but the government allowed the incident to be covered up.

I was in Brasília in the aftermath of Riocentro and asked two key politicians whether they felt Riocentro meant that the security community would get the upper hand and either stop elections or force the proroguing of the existing terms of office, especially that of President Figueiredo. There was widespread speculation and fear in civil society that a *retrocesso* (reversal) of the abertura would occur. Tancredo Neves was surprisingly confident, saying, "The military will have the elections because they need them. Once they have the elections there will be great pressure to respect them. There is no tradition in Brazil for not accepting elections. They will not prorogue mandates because it will completely demoralize the system" (interview, September 8, 1981, Brasília). Senator José Sarney, then president of the progovernment PDS party, was also confident because he felt the legitimacy issue was beginning to affect the military. "They have institutional reasons to leave. As an institution they do not have legitimacy to rule. It is a daily issue for them in their lives. The military do not feel they exercise power in the government. They know they are not ready to take all the hard economic decisions. The technocrats will take them but the military will absorb the responsibility. It is hard to find military officers who accept Delfim's policies. They are often closer to what the middle class think." He also said that he felt the PDS and their allies would select the next president, but if the opposition won it would not create a crisis. He concluded by saying that the "abertura process absolutely needs political parties. We must create alternative institutions of substance." He stressed that the military had to allow the government party more autonomy (interview, September 9, 1981, Brasília).

lup Poll data. An April 1982 poll showed that more than 60 percent of the respondents in the two top socioeconomic groups said the military defended their own interests more than the country's. By a margin of three to one, the same groups called military efforts to promote political morality and end corruption as "bad" or "terrible," as opposed to "excellent" or "good." By the same margin, these groups wanted the next president of Brazil to be a civilian.[9]

Unlike the "fusion" situation of 1970, the military in 1982 faced no cohesion-making armed threat. Rather, as we have seen, the Geisel-Golbery military as government was quite worried about the autonomous growth of the security community, and by 1982 more and more members of the military as institution felt the costs of rule were disturbingly high.

The military had two major institutional interests they wanted to protect if they relinquished direct rule. In speech after speech, military leaders warned against any retaliation (*revanchismo*) against the military. Obviously they felt a proregime civilian would guard against revanchismo, and would leave the vast majority of the state security system intact. The other major interest they had, and which they believed would be preserved under a proregime civilian, was continued national development of the arms industry. Related to this, the military wanted to maintain a strong policy and personnel presence in all state enterprises associated with national security, especially telecommunications, arms, and informatics.[10]

How can we assess the balance of power in Brazil after the elections of 1982? Obviously the military were in a weaker relative position than they were in 1970. Just that. The above statement does *not* necessarily entail that they had less confrontational power than the opposition, or less electoral power than the opposition if the game were played within existing electoral rules. Even after the 1982 elections the military were sanguine that they could control the presidential succession for four reasons. First, they and

---

[9] Data obtained at the headquarters of the Gallup Poll, Brazil, in São Paulo.

[10] I will discuss these industries in Chapter 6.

the state apparatus, unlike the Argentine military and state apparatus after Malvinas, were not in decomposition. And, unlike Argentina in 1982–1983, or Greece in 1974, the military as institution did not perceive the argument for extrication to be so urgent that they would leave power even at the cost of almost certain reprisals by successor governments. Second, as the direct managers of an intact state apparatus, the government leaders believed they had some room for initiative about the rules of the electoral game (which they had in fact modified, without great opposition from civil society, twice in 1981–1982). Third, they saw the succession game as one fundamentally restricted to those members of political society who had votes in the electoral college. They saw political society as being quite distant from civil society, and thus vulnerable to pressure from the state apparatus. Fourth, they came out of the 1982 elections with what they thought was a secure majority in the electoral college; and, unless civil society could prevail upon the state to change the rules and allow a direct election, this was the body that would select the next president.

In their judgment, and in mine, despite the change in the relative balance of power, the absolute balance of power made it reasonable in 1983 to believe that the opposition would not in fact attain the presidency until 1991.

THE END OF THE REGIME

Given the previous argument, why in fact was a leading member of the opposition, Tocredo Neves, scheduled to assume the presidency on March 15, 1985? In theoretical terms my argument for the termination of the authoritarian regime is rather similar to my argument about the fall of democracy in 1964.[11] In my analysis of 1964 I argued that although many factors contributed to the weakening of democratic structures and the sense of crisis, specific (and not overdetermined) political decisions by President Goulart brought about the collapse of the regime. In 1984 the authoritarian regime was also greatly weakened, but, as has just been argued, not in decomposition. Let me make my case as starkly as possible.

[11] Stepan, "Political Leadership and Regime Breakdown: Brazil."

Three interrelated phenomena had to happen for the electoral college endgame to result in the opposition's gaining the presidency in 1985. Politics is seldom parsimonious, but here were the three necessary *and* sufficient causes for the opposition to capture the king:

1. A candidate who had the potential to drive some government supporters to join the opposition had to win the official nomination of the government party.
2. A candidate had to emerge within the opposition who was able both to get the diverse groups to unite (without serious defections or abstentions) behind a single candidate; and to attract sufficient government party members of the electoral college to win a majority.
3. The military (knowing both of the above events might happen) had to allow both the selection of the divisive candidate of the government party and allow the electoral college to meet and vote as scheduled.

Most analysts of Brazil in 1983—myself included— would have said that the possibility of all three of the above happening simultaneously would be extremely unlikely. Certainly none of the three was overdetermined. Why did the unlikely occur? For the empirical and conceptual purposes of this chapter, let me emphasize both political choice and the structural-historical boundaries of choice. Let me also stress that the endgame was a dynamic process in which the military's view of the opposition was changed, and each step completed altered the military's perception of their next possible step.

From the end of May 1984 a number of political actors and analysts began to predict that the opposition would support Tancredo Neves as the unified candidate, Paulo Maluf would get the nomination of the government party, and that Tancredo, aided by votes from the government party, would win unless the military ran the risk of changing the rules, and these analysts doubted that the military would.[12] This possibility must have been seriously

---

[12] I gave a talk advancing this argument at CEDES in Buenos Aires in late May 1984.

considered by the security community. They must have contemplated altering the scenario but not have been able to do so. Why? We are in a realm of conjecture, but most of the conjecture focuses on the interaction of civil society with political society, and of the state with political society. Thus, toward the end of the authoritarian regime, political society—originally the least prestigious actor of the abertura—came center stage.

Here we must return to the dynamics of regime concession and opposition conquest, Juan Linz had stressed that the 1982 election of opposition governors who had just been inaugurated in March 1983 would in fact make the political system a "dyarchy." That is a system with two competing executive power bases with different claims to legitimacy. He said this would inevitably introduce a new dynamic into Brazilian politics, new sources of instability into the regime, and new challenges to the opposition.[13] He was right.

The 1982 election was one of the most intensely fought in Brazil's history. The politicians of both parties looked back over their shoulders at the state, but they also had to look forward to the greatly changed electorate who would increasingly determine their fate and hold them accountable for their actions. In the process of a more competitive campaign, all political parties—even the progovernment PDS—strengthened their national organization and municipal directorates. Cardoso argues that in the process of the 1982 election, the PDS "renewed itself partially and became somewhat more autonomous. This should not be denied. Today there are new leaders who are conservative, but not immobilist."[14]

The nomination of Paulo Maluf—with all the predictable threats this posed for the government's control of the electoral college—was both a testimony to the indefatigable and inventive political qualities of Maluf and to the growing autonomy of even the proregime political society. Ten years of abertura, of strongly contested elections, and the military's public discourse of commit-

---

[13] Juan Linz, "The Transition from an Authoritarian Regime to Democracy in Spain: Some Thoughts for Brazilians."

[14] See Fernando Henrique Cardoso, "Associated-Dependent Development and Democratic Theory."

ment to democracy, opposition, and elections had contributed to some independence of political ambition and some dynamism even within the progovernment party. To this must be added President Figueiredo's ambivalence toward the nomination process, which we will examine later. The impact of the 1982 elections on the opposition was even more dramatic. The newly inaugurated opposition governors in most of Brazil's most powerful states—Franco Montoro in São Paulo, Tancredo Neves in Minas Gerais, and Leonel Brizola in Rio de Janeiro—represented a new stage in the evolution of the opposition. They were opposition leaders not constricted to oratorical tribunes in Brasília. They had electorally sanctioned legitimacy to executive office with some control over municipal and state police. The new governors had great power to convoke (*poder convocatório*) followers to a place for an agenda. The massive 1984 *diretas já* ("direct elections now!") campaign for direct presidential elections is seen as an extraordinary testimony to the resurgence of Brazilian civil society. It was. But, in most of the biggest rallies, the initiation of the event, the order of speakers, the crowd control, and the setting and legitimation of the stage was done by those newly empowered leaders of political society—Governors Montoro, Neves, and Brizola—who, in the process, began to transcend the previous separation of civil and political society and to pool the opposition into a larger, more powerful arena.

After the diretas já campaign, the leaders of political society, especially the opposition governors, emerged as extremely important brokers and mediators of the immensely complicated and intense bargaining that had to be done to produce a unified leader of the opposition. *Veja*, in an excellent special issue devoted to the transition, gives details of the hundreds of intra-elite transactions within political society that occurred while the Tancredo Neves candidacy was crafted.[15] Tancredo Neves's selection required po-

[15] See *Veja*, "Edição Especial : A História Secreta da Sucessão," January 16, 1985, 43. I was in Brazil in May 1984, and in conversations with party leaders such as Franco Montoro, Fernando Henrique Cardoso, and Francisco Weffort I became aware that within each party, major concessions were daily being sought

litical and ideological struggles in the four nongovernmental parties. The selection of a moderate who would not trigger the military's most acute anxiety (revanchismo) was the result of intense negotiations within political society. The willingness and ability of the Brazilian opposition to unite behind a single moderate politician reflect the depth of their collective aspiration to reestablish, as the transcendent task at hand, democratic rule. The realization of this collective aspiration required the capacity of political society to make substantial policy compromises and the deferment of some leaders' personal ambitions to be president.

However, we have to locate our analysis within the larger comparative setting. The latitudinarian qualities of the Brazilian opposition would have been impossible in Chile or Argentina, where the military killed more than one hundred times more people per capita than in Brazil—and killed them more recently. Moreover, in Brazil opposition and government tacitly agreed that the 1979 amnesty was a "mutual amnesty." Thus history allowed the Left, in good conscience, to support a moderate as the necessary price of military extrication.

Finally, why did the military allow the opposition to win? The *Veja* special issue alludes to a series of hard-line efforts linked to the security community to stop the transition. Why were these efforts unsuccessful? Writing so close to the events, my analysis is, of course, necessarily tentative. But five relationships would seem worthy of detailed examination by future historians.

*The Changing Military Perception*
*of "Opposition"*

One issue we need to explore is the changing nature, over time, of what "opposition" meant to the military. The hard-line had said amnesty could not happen because it would be a disaster. It happened in 1979, and the consequences were hardly disastrous.[16] If

---

and agreements crafted. It was a period of intense and creative life within political society.

[16] Senator José Sarney stressed that if we are considering the military's relationship to abertura as a process "amnesty has helped because it did not have a major radicalizing impact on the country" (interview, September 9, 1981, Brasília).

hard-liners had been asked in 1980 if they would accept Leonel Brizola as governor, they would have said, "Absolutely not!" It happened, and nothing happened. By 1984, what "opposition" meant to the military was very complex. They had two institutional requirements. No revanchismo (both Maluf and Tancredo offered assurances, but some military might have felt Tancredo's ability actually to defuse the issue to be greater than Maluf's). The other institutional interest was a strong state and national presence in the informatics and telecommunications industry. As the campaign wore on, it was clear that Tancredo Neves, not Paulo Maluf, was the stronger advocate of a "market reserve" for Brazilian products in these areas. Finally, would a Maluf presidency that would almost certainly polarize the country, or a more consensual Tancredo presidency, be more in the military's long-range interests if what they really wanted was to preclude a hard leftist opposition leader from eventually coming to power?

*The Changing International Context*

The Brazilian military as institution had taken some pride in the fact that they had been less violent and more economically successful than their military colleagues in Uruguay, Argentina, and Chile. However, in 1984 the Uruguayan military were leaving power, and the attempt by Galtieri to stay on by his foreign-policy adventure in Malvinas had led to disaster for the Argentine military as institution. The Brazilian military risked joining Paraguay and Chile if they blocked Tancredo. And they would have to do so under international economic conditions that were so difficult that the costs of governing in a climate of post-diretas já, post-Tancredo fervor would have been extremely high.

*Increasing Legitimacy Concerns*
*within the Military.*

In 1964 there was a Brumairean moment and the overwhelming bulk of the military felt that their actions were legitimate. But 1984 was different. We have already discussed the strong elite preference for a civilian president and why many officers within the rank and file of the military as institution were worried about another term with a military president. To have stopped Tancredo from being president by September 1984 would have required another military president and the imposition of a military solution to Brazil's political future. Moreover, the scandalous events of the Riocentro event in 1981—in which the overwhelming bulk of the military believed the security community was responsible, but in which the military proved internally unable to pursue a serious investigation—probably weakened the military as government's sense of legitimacy to impose a solution, and increased the military as institution's doubts as to whether they had sufficient legitimacy to thwart the upcoming electoral college. The most prestigious figure in military circles, ex-President Ernesto Geisel, held a much publicized two-hour meeting with Tancredo on September 4, 1984, publicly embraced him, and privately assured him that conditions in the military were very unsupportive of a coup.[17]

*Presidential Ambivalence*

João Baptista Figueiredo, as the leader of the military as government, could possibly have imposed a unifying candidate on the PDS in 1983. He was not the king of Spain. He vacillated, he was ambivalent and urged on by close advisors such as SNI chief Octávio Medeiros and Minister Cesar Cals, he occasionally flirted with personal *continuismo*. But, within the tolerable boundaries of the possible, he ultimately elected not to intervene in the selection

---

[17] The photograph was the message. Geisel, normally cool, formal, and distant, is shown in a sport shirt, smiling and embracing Tancredo with both arms. *Veja* argues that Geisel told Tancredo that there was no climate in the army to support any *golpista* adventures, but urged him to have contacts only with those military who were at the ministerial level. Neves left the meeting, according to the *Veja* report, confident that Geisel would lend his moral weight to anti-coup forces. See *Veja*, January 16, 1985, 43.

In the judgment of one active-duty three-star army general, about 90 percent of the army believed that Riocentro was actually the work of the security community. (This fact was never acknowledged by the government investigation.) His rough estimate was that of this 90 percent, one-third felt it was a regrettable "work accident," one-third felt it was reprehensible but did not want to risk splitting the military by pushing for a full investigation and punishment, and one-third were demoralized by the absence of a serious investigation and public sanctions (interview, not for citation, in 1981).

process of his own party, and therefore emerged as an unexpectedly neutral figure.[18]

## The Dahlian Calculus

Given the relatively inactive role of the president, the central question was reduced to whether, under the conditions prevailing in Brazil, the hard-line elements linked to the security community could get sufficient support from the key troop commanders and opinion leaders within the military as institution to mobilize a preventative action. After Tancredo's victory in the electoral college on January 15, 1985, a reversal of this result in the next two months would have constituted a *coup d'état* and required the *de facto* constitution of a new military dictatorship under extremely difficult national and international conditions. For the military as institution the costs of such a course of action must have seemed very high. And, as I have shown on some core issues of concern to the military—the question of revanchismo, the question of the arms-related industries, and the question of Brazil's long-range chances of a moderate center-Left prevailing over a hard-Left— the costs of accepting a Tancredo Neves presidency were not too great. Thus Robert Dahl's famous axiom, "the more the costs of suppression exceed the costs of toleration, the greater the chance for a competitive regime."[19] It would appear that the bulk of the military as institution made a "Dahlian calculation" and decided they would rather take their chances with what would inevitably be a more competitive regime.

[18] For a discussion of the king's role as a critical figure in the Spanish transition, see Linz, "The Transition from an Authoritarian Regime to Democracy in Spain."

[19] Robert A. Dahl, *Polyarchy*, 15. *Veja* reports that as early as the first days of September, Neves met with the hard-line Minister of War, General Walter Pires, and told him that if there were any golpista efforts from any quarter he was prepared to lead an armed-resistance movement. *Veja* provides some details of Tancredo's contingency plans. Even without relying exclusively upon *Veja*'s version, a broad range of indicators makes it reasonable to assume that a coup after September 1984 would not have been bloodless. Two days after his conversation with the Minister of War, Neves had his aforementioned meeting with Geisel. For a discussion of the moves and countermoves concerning a possible coup, see *Veja*, January 16, 1985, 40–45.

# CHAPTER SIX

# The Military in Newly
# Democratic Regimes: the Dimension
# of Military Contestation

AT THE END of any authoritarian regime in which the military had played an important role, a central question is whether the new civilian democratic government will be able to control the military. Of course, this question is part of the larger one of democratic consolidation, but it deserves some independent theoretical, empirical, and political analysis in its own right.

There are many dimensions of the problem of civilian democratic control of the military, but two are of particular saliency. One concerns the *dimension of articulated military contestation* against the policies of the new civilian democratic leadership.[1] The other concerns the *dimension of military institutional prerogatives*, which will be discussed in Chapter 7.

In a democratizing regime the degree of articulated contestation by the military is strongly affected by the extent to which there is intense dispute or substantial agreement between the military and the incoming government concerning a number of key issues. An issue-area of great potential conflict is how the new regime handles the legacy of human-rights violations committed by the previous authoritarian regime. Another issue-area of great potential conflict concerns military reaction toward the democratic government's initiatives vis-à-vis the organizational mission, structure, and control of the military. A third conflict area, which is of course always a point of some contention in any model of civil-military relations, concerns the military budget. However, since

---

[1] I use the word "articulated" to mean clearly and persistently conveyed so as to be intelligible to relevant military and political actors, whether publicly stated or not.

military budget cuts or increases can play a particularly aggravating or ameliorating role in the initial period of a newly democratic regime, they deserve special attention.

Let us begin our comparative empirical analysis by attempting to identify, in very general terms, where the Brazilian New Republic stood concerning the dimension of "articulated conflict" between the military institution and the new democratic regime. For comparative purposes I will present data for the two other bureaucratic-authoritarian regimes that also recently underwent a regime transition, Argentina and Uruguay. The Spanish case, which is especially rich in its theoretical and political implications for Latin America, will also be discussed. By implication, continuing high levels of articulated contestation present threats to the continuing existence of the democratic regime.

## COMPARATIVE LEGACIES OF HUMAN-RIGHTS ABUSES

In all three of the Latin American bureaucratic-authoritarian regimes, prisoners "disappeared" or died while in custody of the armed-forces security apparatus. Thus legal reprisals for human-rights abuses were an issue from which the military wanted to protect themselves after the transition. In quantitative terms, however, the saliency of the issue was least intense in Brazil. On a per capita basis, for every person who disappeared or died in official custody in Brazil, ten died in Uruguay, and over three hundred died in Argentina (see Table 6.1).

At the time of the transition a very different atmosphere toward potential trials existed in each country. In Brazil the Congress in 1979 had voted an amnesty for crimes committed between 1964 and 1979, and this amnesty was widely accepted in both civil and political society as a mutual amnesty. There have been a number of attempts by private individuals and lower courts to press charges against military officers for post-1979 offenses. Most of these met passive resistance and low levels of compliance by military officers. The former number-two military official of the SNI did appear in a civil court on a post-1979 murder charge related to

TABLE 6.1. "Disappearances" in Brazil, Argentina, Uruguay during the Bureaucratic-Authoritarian Regime

|  | Disappeared* | Population in 1975 | Disappeared per 100,000 people |
|---|---|---|---|
| Argentina | 8,960 | 28.0 million | 32.0 |
| Uruguay | 26 | 2.6 million | 1.0 |
| Brazil | 125 | 125.0 million | 0.1 |

* Sources: Argentina: Nunca Más; The Report of the Argentine National Commission on the Disappeared, p. 284. New York: Farrar, Straus, and Giroux, 1986. Brazil: Brasil: Nunca Mais, pp. 291–293. Petropólis: Editora Vozes, 1985. Uruguay: Charles Gillespie, "Party Strategies and Redemocratization: Theoretical and Comparative Perspectives on the Uruguayan Case," p. 460. Ph.D. dissertation, Yale University, 1987.

SNI activities. Nonetheless, three years of civilian rule did not yield one conviction.

In Uruguay, President Sanguinetti and General Medina (the last commander in chief of the army under military rule who Sanguinetti retained as his commander in chief until he reached retirement age in February 1987) had been two of the principal architects of the extrication pact of the Club Naval. Although trials were not an explicit part of the pact, both Sanguinetti and Medina assumed that trials would be kept to a minimum and limited to cases of clear violations of military orders.[2] In December 1986 this implicit agreement was forced to a crisis when the Uruguayan legal system for the first time ordered two former military officers to appear in court to face charges of human-rights offenses. Top military leaders made it clear that they would not enforce court

[2] This is my overall judgment based on personal interviews with high military and political leaders who participated in the Club Naval discussions. The interviews included President Julio María Sanguinetti and General Hugo Medina in Montevideo on February 2 and 3, 1987.

appearances. In order to avoid a military crisis, or a loss of authority, President Sanguinetti, supported by his Colorado party and the majority of the country's second largest party, the Blancos, was able to get, despite the unanimous opposition of the third largest party, the Frente Amplio, sufficient congressional support to pass an amnesty less than a day before the court-appearance date. Even though the military crisis was averted, the agreement was extremely controversial in civil society. In a poll published in Uruguay's most authoritative journal, *Búsqueda*, 65 percent of those polled in Montevideo said they disagreed with the amnesty law.[3] A petition drive for a referendum on the issue began almost immediately.[4]

In Argentina, Raúl Alfonsín campaigned on a human-rights platform, and upon taking office revoked the military's last-minute self-amnesty and announced that he would launch major trials. Despite great resentment and passive and active noncompliance from the officer corps, President Alfonsín was successful in initiating legal proceedings that led to the conviction and imprisonment of eight top junta officials of the 1976–1982 military governments—six for human-rights violations, and two for their conduct of the Malvinas war. This was an unprecedented achievement in Latin American history. However, in the face of increasingly dangerous military opposition he successfully urged Congress in December 1986 to pass a law that put a time limit for new proceedings to be filed. Despite this, a junior-officer barracks mutiny broke out in April 1987.

In Spain approximately 500,000 people died in the Civil War in the 1930s. However, very few deaths had occurred in the last twenty years of Franco, and the issue of trials was never a major contested issue on the transition agenda. In comparative terms, Spain, closely followed by Brazil, experienced the lowest level of conflict over the authoritarian legacy of human-rights abuses. The most intense conflict, and the highest number of convictions, oc-

---

[3] *Búsqueda*, February 26, 1987.

[4] For a detailed discussion of the two-year-long debate over the military amnesty, see Carina Perelli, ''Amnistía sí, amnistía no, amnistía puede ser. . . . ''

curred in Argentina. In Uruguay, the legacy of human-rights abuses produced the only crisis in civil-military relations in the first three years of democracy. The manner of its resolution produced the first challenge of the government's legitimacy from the left.

## MILITARY BUDGETS AND ARMS

The situation in which the least potential conflict exists concerning military budgets would be one where, for whatever reason, the military as institution perceives that the new democratic regime will be somewhat more favorable to their budget needs than the outgoing authoritarian regime, and at the same time the incoming government believes that, in the context of the overall budgetary possibilities, it can increase military budgets.

For Latin America, Brazil approximated the least conflictive position. In the last chapter I mentioned that at least five separate Brazilian active-duty generals and admirals complained forcefully that the military budget had declined sharply since 1974. They specifically argued that the military as institution could more effectively lobby for their legitimate needs if the military as government were not in office. I also mentioned that no officer ever advanced this as an argument for military exit in Chile, Uruguay, or Argentina. The Brazilian military argument seemed counterintuitive; however, at least it was an empirical assertion I could investigate. The Arms Control and Disarmament Agency (ACDA) of the U.S. government reports data that show that Brazil's total military expenditures in U.S. millions of dollars at constant 1982 prices was $2,456 in 1973, $2,050 in 1978, and an estimated $1,698 in 1983.[5]

The absolute decline in Brazilian military expenditures as depicted in the ACDA data is surprising. The data are supported, however, by the Stockholm International Peace Research Institute (SIPRI), which compiles estimates on military expenditures from a variety of different sources. Using different definitions of what

---

[5] ACDA, *World Military Expenditures, 1985*, 55.

they count as military expenditure, and different formulas for inflation adjustment, the International Monetary Fund's *Government Finance Statistics Yearbook*, the Brazilian government's *Anuário Estatístico do Brasil*, and SIPRI's own *World Armament and Disarmament: SIPRI Yearbook* all show an absolute decline in Brazilian military expenditure in the 1970s.[6]

Using ACDA data, how does the Brazilian data on armed-force size and expenditure compare with the other three bureaucratic-authoritarian regimes, Argentina, Chile, and Uruguay? (See Tables 6.2 and 6.3.)

SIPRI, using somewhat different data than ACDA, but with an

TABLE 6.2. Military Expenditures as Percentage of GNP in Four Bureaucratic-Authoritarian Regimes: Argentina, Brazil, Chile, and Uruguay, 1972–1983

| Year | Argentina | Brazil | Chile | Uruguay |
|------|-----------|--------|-------|---------|
| 1972 | 1.4 | 1.4 | 2.3 | 2.4 |
| 1973 | 1.7 | 1.4 | 3.7 | 2.4 |
| 1974 | 1.9 | 1.2 | 4.9 | 2.9 |
| 1975 | 0.8 | 1.1 | 4.8 | 2.7 |
| 1976 | 3.2 | 1.2 | 4.1 | 2.2 |
| 1977 | 3.2 | 1.0 | 4.0 | 2.4 |
| 1978 | 3.0 | 0.8 | 4.2 | 2.3 |
| 1979 | 3.2 | 0.7 | 3.6 | 2.4 |
| 1980 | 3.6 | 0.7 | 3.6 | 2.9 |
| 1981 | 3.9 | 0.7 | 3.7 | 4.0 |
| 1982 | 3.5 | 0.9 | 4.3 | 4.1 |
| 1983 | 2.7 | 0.7 | 4.5 | 3.3 |

*Source*: U.S Government, Arms Control and Disarmament Agency, *World Military Expenditures and Arms Transfers, 1972–1982* (April 1984), 17–49; and *World Military Expenditures and Arms Transfers, 1985* (August 1985), 52–88.

[6] See SIPRI *Yearbook, 1983*, 188.

effort at internally consistent methodology, has compiled comparative data for twenty-three Latin American countries for the period 1974 to 1982. According to SIPRI, Brazil, which in 1976 spent twice as much of its Gross Domestic Product (GDP) on military expenses as did Mexico, by 1981 shared with Mexico the lowest ratio of military expenditures to GDP in all of Latin America. Astoundingly, if the very preliminary estimates for the Malvinas crisis year of 1982 are subsequently confirmed, in that year Chile spent over fourteen times as much of its GDP on military expenditures than did Brazil, Argentina almost ten times as much, and Uruguay almost six times as much (see Table 6.4). Finally, using the same SIPRI data, let us contrast the Brazilian military expendi-

TABLE 6.3. Armed-Force Size in Four Bureaucratic-Authoritarian Regimes: Argentina, Brazil, Chile, and Uruguay, 1972–1983

| | Armed Forces (in thousands) | | | | Armed Forces per 1,000 people | | | |
|---|---|---|---|---|---|---|---|---|
| Year | Ar. | Br. | Ch. | Ur. | Ar. | Br. | Ch. | Ur. |
| 1972 | 140 | 410 | 75 | 20 | 5.7 | 4.1 | 7.7 | 7.1 |
| 1973 | 160 | 420 | 75 | 20 | 6.5 | 4.1 | 7.6 | 7.1 |
| 1974 | 150 | 435 | 90 | 25 | 6.0 | 4.1 | 9.0 | 8.9 |
| 1975 | 160 | 455 | 110 | 25 | 6.3 | 4.2 | 10.8 | 8.9 |
| 1976 | 155 | 450 | 111 | 28 | 6.0 | 4.1 | 10.7 | 8.9 |
| 1977 | 155 | 450 | 111 | 28 | 5.9 | 4.0 | 10.6 | 9.7 |
| 1978 | 155 | 450 | 111 | 28 | 5.8 | 3.9 | 10.4 | 9.7 |
| 1979 | 155 | 450 | 111 | 28 | 5.7 | 3.8 | 10.3 | 9.7 |
| 1980 | 155 | 450 | 116 | 28 | 5.6 | 3.7 | 10.5 | 9.7 |
| 1981 | 155 | 450 | 116 | 28 | 5.4 | 3.6 | 10.4 | 9.7 |
| 1982 | 175 | 460 | 116 | 29 | 6.0 | 3.6 | 10.3 | 10.0 |
| 1983 | 175 | 460 | 126 | 30 | 5.9 | 3.5 | 11.0 | 10.3 |

*Source*: U.S Government, Arms Control and Disarmament Agency, *World Military Expenditures and Arms Transfers, 1972–1982*, and *1985*, 17–49, and 52–88.

tures as a percentage of GDP with those of the major democracies of the world outside of Latin America (see Table 6.5).

Attention should be brought at this time to the fact that the 1982 figures presented in Tables 6.4 and 6.5 for Brazil (0.6 percent), Costa Rica (0.7 percent), and Mexico (0.5 percent) represent the three lowest figures for *all* 117 nations on which SIPRI collects data. With the possible exceptions of countries like Iceland and Barbados, for whom SIPRI does not report data, this makes Brazil the "democracy" with the lowest level of military expenditures as a percentage of GDP in the world, and the nation with the second-lowest level of all major nations in the world.[7]

What can we say about the implications of the data contained in these six tables? From the perspective of basic human needs of the poor and the survival of the species, world expenditures for weapons of destruction are too high. However, in purely comparative terms, the Brazilian military budgetary situation at the end of the authoritarian regime was reasonably auspicious, both for the Brazilian military and for the New Republic. Auspicious for the military because in comparison to the other bureaucratic-authoritarian regimes, military expenses were low enough so that there were no great societal pressures to slash them. Auspicious for the new civilian regime because the new regime by comparative world

[7] Skeptics will of course challenge the data. They will say that the Brazilian military "disguised" a lot of their costs. The two major sources of hidden expenditures are the annual "special credits" that are given to the military, and the extensive expenses listed under nonmilitary research and development or industrial research expenses that are in fact related to the arms industries. For the sake of argument, let us make two major assumptions. First, that even though the best estimate of Brazilian military expenditures is that 70 percent is spent on personnel (where costs are relatively difficult to disguise), we should nonetheless assume that the Brazilian military spends twice as much as the ACDA data indicate. The second assumption is that in Chile, Argentina, and Uruguay there have been *absolutely no* hidden military expenditures, so we will accept the ACDA data as is. Even if we made these two assumptions, Brazil in 1981, according to the ACDA calculations (shown in Table 6.2), would have spent only 1.4 percent of its GNP on military expenditures, compared to 3.9 percent in Argentina, 3.7 percent in Chile, and 4.0 percent in Uruguay. If we use SIPRI estimates, Argentina, Chile, and Uruguay would have spent even higher proportions on military-related expenses. See *SIPRI Yearbook, 1984*, 127–131.

TABLE 6.4. Latin American Military Expenditures as a Percentage of Gross Domestic Product: SIPRI Data

| | 1976 | 1977 | 1978 | 1979 | 1980 | 1981 | 1982 | 1983 | 1984 |
|---|---|---|---|---|---|---|---|---|---|
| CENTRAL AMERICA | | | | | | | | | |
| Costa Rica | 0.7 | 0.8 | 0.7 | 0.7 | 0.7 | 0.7 | 0.8 | 0.8 | (0.8) |
| Cuba | .. | 8.3 | 8.3 | 8.5 | 7.8 | 8.0 | 9.2 | 8.6 | 9.8 |
| Dominican Republic | 1.7 | 1.7 | 1.8 | 2.0 | 1.5 | [1.7] | [1.6] | 1.5 | [1.5] |
| El Salvador | 1.7 | 2.0 | 2.1 | (2.0) | 2.8 | 3.7 | 4.4 | 4.4 | 4.9 |
| Guatemala | 1.5 | 1.5 | 1.7 | 1.7 | 1.8 | 1.9 | [2.4] | (2.6) | (2.9) |
| Haiti | 1.2 | 1.2 | 1.3 | 1.4 | 1.4 | 1.5 | 1.6 | 1.7 | .. |
| Honduras | 1.8 | 1.9 | 2.3 | 2.3 | (3.5) | (4.5) | [5.0] | [5.7] | (6.0) |
| Jamaica | 2.2 | 2.6 | 2.9 | 2.9 | 2.9 | (3.2) | [3.0] | [3.0] | [2.8] |
| Mexico | 0.6 | 0.6 | 0.5 | 0.5 | 0.6 | 0.6 | 0.6 | [0.7] | [0.6] |
| Nicaragua | 2.1 | 2.5 | 3.2 | [3.1] | 4.4 | [5.0] | (5.9) | (9.6) | [11.7] |
| Panama | 1.7 | [1.5] | [1.5] | [1.5] | [1.2] | [1.2] | [1.3] | [1.4] | .. |
| Trinidad and Tobago | 1.5 | 1.4 | 2.3 | 1.9 | 1.9 | 2.2 | 3.2 | .. | .. |

SOUTH AMERICA

| | | | | | | | | | |
|---|---|---|---|---|---|---|---|---|---|
| Argentina | 2.4 | 2.4 | 2.7 | 2.5 | 2.6 | 2.9 | [5.9] | (3.9) | [3.3] |
| Bolivia | 3.8 | 3.3 | 3.5 | 3.5 | (3.7) | (4.9) | (4.8) | [3.8] | [4.0] |
| Brazil | 1.3 | 1.1 | 0.9 | 0.8 | 0.5 | 0.6 | 0.6 | (0.8) | [0.7] |
| Chile | 6.1 | 6.9 | 6.4 | 6.2 | 7.4 | 6.5 | [8.7] | [9.5] | [8.8] |
| Colombia | (1.2) | . . | (1.6) | (1.8) | 2.0 | 1.8 | 1.8 | 2.2 | 2.0 |
| Ecuador | 2.2 | 3.1 | 2.1 | 2.0 | 1.9 | (1.9) | (1.6) | (1.7) | [1.8] |
| Guyana | 8.8 | 6.0 | (5.3) | (5.1) | [6.5] | 6.0 | 7.5 | [9.8] | [9.2] |
| Paraguay | 1.7 | 1.6 | 1.5 | 1.3 | 1.4 | 1.5 | (1.6) | (1.5) | . . |
| Peru | 5.0 | 7.3 | 5.5 | 3.9 | (5.7) | (7.2) | (7.2) | (8.6) | [8.2] |
| Uruguay | 2.2 | 2.3 | 2.6 | (2.9) | 2.6 | 3.4 | [4.3] | . . | . . |
| Venezuela | 2.2 | 2.2 | 2.1 | 2.4 | 2.7 | 3.1 | 3.4 | 2.9 | (3.1) |

*Source: Stockholm International Peace Research Institute, World Armaments and Disarmament: SIPRI Yearbook, 1984, 129–131.*
*Note: Cuban figures represent percentages of Gross Material Product.*
*Conventions:*
  . . Information not available or not applicable
  ( ) Uncertain data
  [ ] Estimates with a high degree of uncertainty

TABLE 6.5. Military Expenditures as a Percentage of Gross Domestic Product for Brazil and the Major Non-Latin American Democracies, 1976–1985

| | 1976 | 1977 | 1978 | 1979 | 1980 | 1981 | 1982 | 1983 | 1984 | 1985 |
|---|---|---|---|---|---|---|---|---|---|---|
| Brazil | 1.3 | 1.1 | 0.9 | 0.8 | 0.5 | 0.6 | 0.6 | (0.8) | [0.7] | [0.8] |
| India | 3.2 | 3.0 | 2.9 | 3.1 | 3.1 | 3.1 | 3.3 | 3.2 | — | — |
| Japan | 0.9 | 0.9 | 0.9 | 0.9 | 0.9 | 0.9 | 1.0 | 1.0 | — | — |
| NATO | | | | | | | | | | |
| Canada | 1.8 | 1.9 | 2.0 | 1.8 | 1.8 | 1.8 | 2.1 | 2.0 | 2.1 | 2.2 |
| USA | 5.4 | 5.3 | 5.1 | 5.1 | 5.6 | 5.8 | 6.5 | 6.7 | 6.5 | 6.6 |
| Belgium | 3.1 | 3.2 | 3.3 | 3.3 | 3.3 | 3.5 | 3.4 | 3.1 | 3.1 | 3.3 |
| Denmark | 2.3 | 2.3 | 2.3 | 2.3 | 2.4 | 2.5 | 2.5 | 2.4 | 2.3 | 2.3 |
| France | 3.8 | 3.9 | 4.0 | 3.9 | 4.0 | 4.2 | 4.1 | 4.2 | 4.1 | 4.1 |
| FR Germany | 3.5 | 3.4 | 3.3 | 3.3 | 3.3 | 3.4 | 3.4 | 3.4 | 3.3 | 3.3 |
| Greece | 6.9 | 7.0 | 6.7 | 6.3 | 5.7 | 7.0 | 6.9 | 6.3 | 7.2 | 7.1 |
| Italy | 2.3 | 2.4 | 2.4 | 2.4 | 2.4 | 2.5 | 2.6 | 2.7 | 2.7 | 2.7 |
| Luxembourg | 0.8 | 0.8 | 0.8 | 0.8 | 0.9 | 0.9 | 0.8 | 0.9 | 0.9 | 0.9 |

| | | | | | | | | | | |
|---|---|---|---|---|---|---|---|---|---|---|
| Netherlands | 3.2 | 3.3 | 3.1 | 3.2 | 3.1 | 3.2 | 3.2 | 3.2 | 3.2 | 3.1 |
| Norway | 3.1 | 3.1 | 3.2 | 3.1 | 2.9 | 2.9 | 3.0 | 3.1 | 2.8 | 3.2 |
| Portugal | 4.0 | 3.5 | 3.5 | 3.5 | 3.5 | 3.5 | 3.4 | 3.4 | 3.3 | 3.2 |
| United Kingdom | 4.8 | 4.7 | 4.5 | 4.6 | 5.0 | 4.8 | 5.0 | 5.3 | 5.3 | 5.4 |
| OTHER EUROPE | | | | | | | | | | |
| Austria | 1.2 | 1.2 | 1.3 | 1.3 | 1.2 | 1.2 | 1.2 | 1.4 | 1.2 | 1.4 |
| Finland | 1.4 | 1.4 | 1.4 | 1.4 | 1.5 | 1.5 | 1.7 | (1.7) | (1.6) | (1.3) |
| Ireland | 1.8 | 1.7 | 1.7 | 1.8 | 1.9 | 1.8 | 1.8 | 1.7 | — | — |
| Spain | 1.8 | 1.7 | 1.7 | 1.7 | 1.9 | 1.9 | 2.2 | 2.3 | 2.4 | 2.4 |
| Sweden | 3.2 | 3.3 | 3.3 | 3.3 | 3.2 | 3.3 | 3.2 | 3.1 | 3.0 | 2.9 |
| Switzerland | 2.3 | 2.1 | 2.1 | 2.2 | 2.1 | 2.0 | 2.1 | 2.0 | 2.1 | 2.2 |
| MIDDLE EAST | | | | | | | | | | |
| Israel | (26.4) | (24.4) | (20.4) | (20.1) | (20.3) | (20.3) | [19.2] | [20.8] | [17.9] | — |

*Source:* Stockholm International Peace Research Institute, *World Armaments and Disarmament: SIPRI Yearbook, 1986*, 243–247.

*Conventions:*

— Information not available or not applicable
( ) Uncertain data
[ ] Estimates with a high degree of uncertainty

standards had a very low military expenditure to Gross National Product (GNP) ratio and was not immediately forced into an intense, articulated conflict with the military over grossly inflated expenditures. In fact, the rank-and-file officers and soldiers in distant garrisons, and, indeed, many leaders of the military as institution, felt the authoritarian regime had rather neglected their needs; they did not perceive a major budgetary imperative to maintain the authoritarian regime, and some key leaders even thought they would fare better as a budgetary pressure group under a democratic regime. The first two years of the New Republic proved them right as the military budget percentage of GNP rose somewhat, and all three services launched significant modernization programs, which the government allowed in order to help turn military attention to professional technical concerns as well as to avoid conflict with the military.

The situation in Argentina was virtually the opposite to that in Brazil. The Ministry of Defense estimates that the combined expenses of the defense sector were 5.6 percent of GNP in 1981 and that they were reduced to 3 percent in 1985.[8]

This sharp reduction was perceived by the military as ''unpatriotic'' because of their perceived need to have sufficient resources to pose a credible military threat to the British in the South Atlantic theater. The military also argued that the combination of lower military salaries and the attacks on the military as an institution caused a crisis of morale. Frequent mention was made of the fact that officers had to take a second job to make ends meet and that applications to the military academy plunged.

In Uruguay the situation was structurally closer to that of Argentina than to that of Brazil. The government announced a plan to reduce military expenditures. However, the situation was significantly less conflictual than Argentina because the reductions were being done more slowly and there was no military sense of a need to rebuild against an external enemy as there was in post-Malvinas Argentina. Also, the sense of conflict between the government and the military was muted by the constant contact and mutual respect between President Sanguinetti and his co-architect

---

[8] Figures supplied to the author by the Argentine Ministry of Defense.

of the Pacto del Club Naval, General Medina. Medina, the most powerful figure in the Uruguayan Army in the period before and after the military left government, insisted that the army would weather the transition in a reasonably good state of readiness and morale, while his counterparts in Argentina argued precisely the opposite.

If applications to military academies are an indicator of comparative prestige, the difference between pre- and post-transition in Uruguay and Argentina is striking. In 1980 and 1981 the Uruguayan military academy received a total of 503 applications. In 1985 and 1986 applications had increased to 791, and the director was reasonably sanguine that applications were not a problem despite the fact that the military no longer controlled the government.[9] In Argentina the situation was sharply different. In 1980 and 1981 the Argentine military academy received a total of 1,727 applications. In 1985 and 1986 the total number of applications had plummeted to 857, and the director of the academy said that, due to a decline in qualified applicants, the school was operating at only one-half its capacity.[10]

The Spanish situation was surprisingly close to that in Brazil. The military share of the central government expenses in 1945–1946 (non-GNP) was 54 percent. By 1972–1974 it was in the 22–24 percent range.[11] A widespread perception inside and outside the military was that the military was a "neglected cousin" by the end of the Franco regime.[12] In 1974–1975 military expenditures as a percentage of GNP in Spain were 1.7 percent; in 1985 they were 2.4 percent.[13]

[9] Figures supplied to the author by General Washington A. Varela, director of the Military Academy, on February 2, 1987, in Montevideo.

[10] "Decrece en un Cincuenta Porciento la Vocación por Seguir la Carrera Militar," *La Razón*, July 18, 1986. Raw data on applications from 1980 to 1986 supplied to the author by the Ministry of Defense, which confirmed the assertions of the director of the Colegio Militar reported by *La Razón*.

[11] Rafael Bañón y José Antonio Olmeda, "Las Fuerzas Armadas en España: Institucionalización y Proceso de Cambio," 307.

[12] See Manuel Gonzales, "Las Fuerzas Armadas: Pariente Pobre del Régimen de Franco."

[13] Spanish data from ACDA, *World Military Expenditures, 1984*, and *1985*.

## MILITARY ARMS SUPPLY

The question of the supply of arms is closely related to the issue of budgets, and in those cases where a country imports all its weapons "military arms supply" is in fact completely subsumed by the budget debate. However, if there is a major debate in the country about the size, direction, content, and control of a domestic military-industrial complex, then it becomes an issue that requires separate analytic and political attention. Here again the Brazilian data are surprising. The Brazilian military regime passed through three distinct phases in its conscious effort to build up a more autonomous military-industrial complex. From 1964 to 1967 the private industrial federation of São Paulo (FIESP), in consultation with the military authorities, created a Permanent Group for Industrial Mobilization (GPMI) that focused explicitly on forging an arms industry. This was of mutual interest because at the time there was great excess capacity in the depressed Brazilian economy. The GPMI was explicitly supported by the air force's Center for Aerospace Technology (CTA), the army's Institute of Military Engineering, and the navy's Center of Marine Research. In the second phase (1967–1975) of the development of the Brazilian military-industrial complex, the air force, in 1969, created an industrial firm (EMBRAER) for the manufacture of military and commercial airplanes. The Army Ministry, working closely with the two national private industries ENGESA and Bernardini, extended Brazil's extensive automobile-and truck-making capacity into the field of armored personnel carriers and light tanks, which had particularly good suspension systems. The navy, working with Brazil's large and underutilized shipbuilding industry, began to build ships.

The third major phase of the Brazilian arms industry began around 1975 with state holding companies working closely with the National Security Council, the Foreign Ministry, and the National Industrial Confederation to mount a heavily subsidized, but internationally competitive, arms-export industry.[14]

---

[14] The above account and periodization are based on the best source on this story (which is more complex than I could convey in a few pages). See Brigagão, *O*

Brazil exported virtually no arms in 1970. By the early 1980s the claim was frequently made that if services were included, Brazil was the fifth largest arms exporter in the world. John Hoyt Williams went so far as to assert that "at least forty nations are importing Brazilian military goods, and Brasília's forecast of $3 billion in military sales is perhaps on the conservative side."[15] Whatever the exact details (and much dispute, self-serving exaggeration, subsidies, and great secrecy in this area do exist), it is clear that the Brazilian military emerged from the bureaucratic-authoritarian regime with one of the most powerful arms industries in the Third World and as the only Latin American country with a significant arms-export industry at all. According to ACDA, between 1980 and 1983 Brazil accounted for 94.4 percent of the arms exports of Brazil, Chile, Argentina, and Uruguay combined.[16]

Once again, what are the implications of this for our task at hand? Is the Brazilian arms industry a source of articulated conflict between the military as an institution and the new democratic regime? A key point that needs to be recognized is that nonmilitary industrialists, both domestic and foreign, are a major component in the military-industrial complex. Clóvis Brigagão estimates that 50 Brazilian firms directly produce military equipment, that 350–400 firms supply parts, and that 200,000 people are involved in the arms industry.[17] Hoyt estimates that half of the major firms are in the private sector.[18] ENGESA is headed by a civilian, and as de Barros notes, "the [1982] decision of the Army Ministry to fire the president of IMBEL (a four-star general) and replace him with

---

*Mercado da Segurança*, esp. 15–68. For an excellent assessment of the evolution of the arms industry from the viewpoint of military strategy, see Alexandre de S. C. Barros, "Brazil." See also John Hoyt Williams, "Brazil: Giant of the Southern Cone," and his "Brazil: A New Giant in the Arms Industry."

[15] Williams, "Brazil: A New Giant in the Arms Industry," 26. Brazil was ranked as one of the ten largest suppliers of arms to the Third World in both the 1979–1982 and the 1983–1986 reports of the U.S. Congressional Research Service. See *The New York Times*, May 19, 1987, p. A9.

[16] ACDA, *World Military Expenditures, 1985*, 94–130.

[17] Brigagão, *O Mercado da Segurança*, 47.

[18] Williams, "Brazil: A New Giant in the Arms Industry," 25.

a civilian engineer (the president of ENGESA) seems to have represented an Army drive for greater efficiency.''[19]

Let us directly address the question of the impact of this huge military-industrial complex on the future of democracy. I want to advance a heretical argument. One of the indirect background reasons that makes Third World armies so eager to control the governments of their countries (they normally do so in more than a third of the countries) is that they are acutely aware that they are almost totally dependent on the importation of foreign arms *and* they have no significant internal civilian constituency with a structurally vested interest in arms importation or domestic arms development and production.[20] This thus can become a military justification or motivation for controlling the government and the nation's budget. If one accepts this argument, then the creation of a massive national arms-producing and exporting industry involving hundreds of civilian firms with a permanent structural interest in arms production weakens one of the significant and distinctive rationales for dependent Third World armies to assume direct power. With an increased arms-producing capacity and the development of a strong constituency in civil society politically articulating their interests, this major arms buildup is politically defused—and even gains some legitimacy— precisely because of the powerful export dimensions in the normal context of balance-of-payment problems. In the particular case of Brazil, the presence of a massive arms-producing and exporting capacity means that some of the ideological and industrial infra-structure arguments the military could conceivably utilize as a reason for seizing control of the government are lessened.

From this perspective Brazil's military-industrial complex may

[19] de Barros, ''Brazil,'' 81.

[20] I say ''indirect background'' reasons because the literature on military coups does not identify the absence of an arms industry as a direct motivation for military coups. However, the military in developing countries frequently argue that they are the only group in society who do anything constructive about the question of external defense capacity. This historic self-image is particularly strong in Latin America, where the military maintain that they were the core of the independence movement and, therefore, of the nation-state itself.

paradoxically strengthen the chances for democracy. There is, however, a major policy issue for democratic theory and practice. Virtually all major Western democracies have a military-industrial complex. But the question these raise is *not* that they directly threaten to overthrow the government. Rather, the serious question for democratic theory and practice is: How can political society *control* these complexes so that they do not misallocate resources and threaten peace? These are major problems in all Western democracies—especially the United States—but it is a different problem than those faced by Third World polities with dependent, insecure militaries. Brazil now has a serious issue for the democratic practice of control, but I suggest that Brazil along with India are possibly the only Third World countries where the issue of a domestic arms-production capacity is more one of control and direction than of threats to the existence of a democratic regime, per se.

In Argentina the situation was much more conflictual. The arms industry had traditionally been virtually one-hundred percent controlled by the military in their Fabricaciones Militares. The Alfonsín government transferred all the military industries from the direct control of the military to the civilian-controlled Ministry of Defense that it had established. It encouraged further military suspicions when it attempted to privatize or close some of the most inefficient components of the arms industry as part of its larger policy to reduce the budget deficit of the central government.

In Uruguay there was no significant tradition of a military or a civilian arms industry, so the arms industry was not a conflict issue for the new democratic government in itself, but was subsumed as part of the previously discussed budgetary debate.

The Spanish situation is closer structurally and politically to the Brazilian situation. In 1972 Franco set up a state holding company (Defex, S.A.), made up of five public and seven private companies, to promote arms production. Given the large-scale military modernization program begun under the democratic regime, the Spanish military-industrial complex grew rapidly, by 1984 ranking twelfth in the world in production, generating 60,000 jobs, with thirty Spanish firms participating in the arms-export market.[21] In 1986, with the strong support of the socialist government, the Spanish people voted in a referendum in favor of NATO participation. As Spain modernizes its military to conform to NATO standards, domestic suppliers will almost certainly grow.

## ORGANIZATIONAL MISSION, STRUCTURE, and CONTROL OF THE MILITARY

Conflicts over the military mission will be most intense if the new civilian government wants to restructure the military's mission, and establish strong control mechanisms, while the military sees such policy initiatives as threatening.

From 1964 to 1985 a major part of the professional identification of the leaders of the Brazilian military, especially the army, had been supplied by their role as direct managers of the polity and their struggle against internal enemies. Theorists both inside and outside of the military have worried about the "crisis of mission" the Brazilian military would experience when and if they left power. This lack of professional mission was seen as a dangerous destabilizing force that would motivate them to reconquer government.

The extraordinary expansion of Brazil's role in the world economy, the Malvinas war, the Brazilian military's extensive involvement in Surinam, and the growth of the arms-export industry may, however, have reduced the threat by giving the military a sense of multiple missions. The Brazilian military, especially the navy, is increasingly aware that Brazil has economic and political interests throughout the world, a major commercial shipping activity, and one of the longest coastlines in the world. However, naval leaders frequently argue that Brazil has almost no military capacity to project its power, and to protect its interests, on a global scale. It is a matter of common knowledge that when South Africa attacked Angola, Cuba came to the defense of Angola with arms. What is often forgotten is that the Geisel government, with its strategic interest in Angolan oil, was one of the first countries in the world

[21] See Stanley G. Payne, "Modernization of the Armed Forces," 189–191.

to recognize Angola, and that at the same time that Cuba was sending arms, Brazil dispatched three ships, laden with food, to feed the besieged Marxist government in Luanda.[22] The Malvinas war was a disaster for the Argentine military. The post-Malvinas trials initially stiffened the Chilean military's resolve to retain power. The Brazilian military, however, "read" Malvinas quite differently, and in ways that could possibly help democracy.

The biggest impression Malvinas made on them was that the Argentine military, since it had organized itself to dominate internal enemies, was completely unprepared to fight a major international power. They were particularly struck by Argentina's total incapacity for combined army, navy, and air force actions to sustain sufficient logistical support to wage a medium-intensity war. Upon reflection they realized that they, too, have almost no professional training or logistical capacity to operate a joint task force under conditions similar to those Argentina faced. In addition, they privately recognized that Argentina displayed some military capacity Brazil did not know it possessed and that Brazil did not possess. The interest in increasing purely military professionalism in post-Malvinas Brazil is clearly much stronger than before, and has worked toward resolving the military-mission identity crisis.[23]

Finally, the fact that Brazil exports arms to forty countries in the world opens up a whole range of lucrative foreign military-advising and mission roles for Brazil's military corps. Under the aegis of Brazil's excellent and aggressive professional foreign service (Itamaraty) arms deliveries to conflict-ridden or oil-rich countries will be used to gain a strategic foothold for Brazil in new markets.

[22] Stumpf and Pereira Filho, *A Segunda Guerra*, 82–84. For an informed account of Brazil's complex worldwide geopolitical strategy, see Wayne A. Selcher, *Brazil's Multilateral Relations: Between First and Third Worlds*, esp. 105–144 and 213–244. For a strong advocacy by a progressive civilian that Brazil should build up its navy and virtually nonexistent coast guard, see Hermano Alves, "A Insegurança Nacional," *Afinal*, June 18, 1985, 19.

[23] For an extensive documentation and bibliography concerning mission diversification in the Brazilian military, see Stanley Hilton, "The Brazilian Military."

To respond to this new environment and new possibilities, all three branches of the Brazilian military unveiled, in the first two years of civilian rule, complex new modernization plans. These plans involved both new equipment and force restructuring that would help them respond to what they saw as the "lessons learned" by the Malvinas conflict. The army launched a "Força Terrestre 1990" (Land Force 1990 plan) whose goal was to achieve greater operational capacity.[24] The navy announced new initiatives for nuclear-powered submarines, and the air force announced a program to develop new air-to-air missiles, telecommunication satellites, and a new generation of jet fighters.[25]

These plans did not cause any significant conflict with the new civilian government partly because, as we have seen, military expenditures by world standards had been low. Just as important, there was no conflict because all these plans were designed not by the new civilian government but by the military themselves, and the Sarney government and the legislature accepted them without discussion. Thus, there was low-articulated conflict due to high accommodation on the part of the new government. The accommodation is partly explained by the civilian desire to see military attention turned to more conventional external defense missions. The absence of conflict concerning control of the military is also due to the fact that the Sarney government did not carry out, propose, or indeed even publicly speculate about any new ways for civilians to increase their control of the military.

Unlike the virtual complete accommodation on the part of the Sarney government, in Argentina President Alfonsín made a major initiative concerning the control of the military. The Ministry

---

[24] This plan had three components: first, a territorial reorganization into seven commands with special emphasis on rapid-response forces and new garrisons on Brazil's northern tier; second, substantial infusions of largely Brazilian-made equipment such as armed personnel carriers, land-to-air missiles, troop-carrier helicopters, and new electronic systems; third, upgrading of conventional professional education.

[25] See "Militares: Troca de Poder," *Veja*, October 16, 1985; "Modernização do Exército Até '90 Custa CR$ 1 Trilhão," *Jornal do Brazil*, December 15, 1985; and "Forças Armadas Estabelecem Modernização Como Meta," *Folha de São Paulo*, April 13, 1986.

of Defense was reestablished, and a civilian was placed in control and given major responsibility for the military budget. A Joint General Staff of the armed forces was to be made dependent on the Minister of Defense, and to assume progressively the task of military planning, a task that had traditionally been carried out by the army, navy, and air force commanders acting independently. The peak intelligence agency, SIDE, was put in civilian hands and restructured. A team in which civilians were predominant was placed in charge of reorganizing military ideology, curriculum, and mission. A civilian was made director of the Escuela de Defensa Nacional, the Argentine equivalent of the Brazilian Escola Superior de Guerra.[26]

The bold Alfonsín initiatives would have met with passive resistance in the best of circumstances; they in fact engendered widespread military resentment because of the overall context of trials of military officers. Conflict was further intensified by substantial budgetary cuts, which prevented the military from realizing their desire to construct a credible threat against British control of the Malvinas, and by the limited preparation of civil and political society for the task of planning and directing military affairs.

In this context there has in fact been little of the professional strategic and tactical modernization that both Alfonsín and the Argentine military agreed was necessary after the Malvinas disgrace. Thus after three years of civilian rule, and a halving of the military budget, almost all of Argentina's old military units are still in existence; many of them are headed by commanders who express sentiments of humiliation and anger because their units are shrunken and in a poor state of operational readiness. If many of the nonoperating units had been abolished and some new highly mobile command established, Alfonsín and the military could have said that some modernization had occurred.

The situation in Uruguay is remarkably different from that of

---

[26] The most detailed and careful treatment of these reforms is found in Andrés Fontana, "Fuerzas Armadas y Consolidación Democrática en Argentina." Fontana is preparing a book that will contain most of the central documents concerning the reform initiative, *Los Militares y Alfonsín: Una Relación Conflictiva*. Also see C. J. Moneta, "Fuerzas Armadas y Gobierno Constitucional."

Brazil or Argentina. The president has appointed a civilian Minister of Defense. The formal control of military intelligence has been passed to the Minister of Defense. The legislature reviews in great detail military budgets and publishes the discussions. The Ministry of Defense and his subsecretary routinely appear before the legislature to answer questions. The president and the Congress exercise effective control over senior military promotions. Like Brazil, conflict has been avoided—with the extremely important exception of the already discussed issue of military trials—by accommodation, but in the Uruguayan case the accommodation has been done by the military.

Concerning force structure and threat perception, the president, the Secretary of Defense, and the military minister have collaborated closely to jointly create greater attention to an external defense mission and to develop greater technical capacity to carry out this mission. For the top military and governing authorities alike, the most realistic "hypothesis of war" is a Brazilian or Argentine invasion. The only realistic goal for the military and the government is to put up a symbolic defense that is of sufficient "ethical quality" to justify the support of an external ally (Brazil or Argentina), and to be sufficiently trained technically to use the equipment given by the allies.[27]

In Spain the "neglected cousin" status of a large but poorly equipped military meant that there was reasonable agreement among important sections of the military and the leaders of the transition that a gradual modernization of the armed forces should be a joint goal. The decision to join NATO, as a way of joining Europe, also gave political and military leaders some common ground. The training and equipment reorganization to approach NATO standards inevitably means a military institution in-

---

[27] In surprising common terms this general description of Uruguay's new training program was spelled out to me in separate interviews with the president of Uruguay, Julio María Sanguinetti; the Minister of Defense, Dr. Juan Vicente Chiarino; the director of the Military Academy and former chief of army intelligence, General Virela Washington; and the former commander in chief of the army, General Hugo Medina, in Montevideo on February 2–3, 1987.

creasingly structured for external rather than internal defense missions.

In the first ten years of the transition there was a slow but gradual creation of a new model of civilian control of the military. In 1977, for the first time in Spain's history, a Minister of Defense position was created and the three service heads lost their place in the Cabinet. However, in the critical period of creating the office, the incumbent was an active-duty army officer, General Gutiérrez Mellado. Rather like General Medina in Uruguay, General Gutiérrez Mellado, aided greatly by the king, acted in a critical period of the transition as an effective broker between a cautious democratic government and a wary military. Even before the advent of the socialist government, following national elections in November 1982, the first civilian Minister of Defense had assumed office.

Despite the support of the king and General Gutiérrez Mellado, the new constitution of 1978 and the new code of military justice of 1980, both of which reduced military prerogatives, were subjects of serious criticism in military circles.

Spain, unlike Brazil, Uruguay, or Argentina, did have a major problem of insurgence and terrorism. The guerrilla forces in the Basque area often inflamed military and right-wing sentiment. Not one army officer was killed during the Basque terrorist activity in the 1968–1975 Franco period, or in the 1975–1977 transition. But in the postelectoral period of democratic rule between 1978–1987, thirty-seven army officers died.[28] The combination of nonrecognition of the flag or the monarchy by some political parties, the slow curtailment of military legal privileges, and, most important, the Basque insurgency, created a fertile atmosphere for coup plots and counterplots. The February 23, 1981, coup attempt, during which much of the government was held hostage in the Cortes, was in fact only one of three plots that were being formed. The role of the king in personally assuming command of the anti-coup

[28] Juan Linz and Alfred Stepan, "Political Crafting of Democratic Consolidation or Destruction: European and South American Comparisons." For a more detailed analysis of how the new Spanish democracy handled Basque violence, see Robert P. Clark, *The Basque Insurgents: ETA, 1952–1980*, esp. 126–139.

forces was decisive in preserving democracy and allowing trials and imprisonment of the officers involved to follow.[29]

In terms of our analysis there certainly was civil-military tension over the Basque case, but it is also important to stress that military sentiment was divided over what should be the correct policy-response of the government. The members of the army high command did not articulate explicit opposition to the government's strategy vis-à-vis the terrorists.

If we examined only the dimension of articulated goal conflict, the Spanish and Brazilian civilian governments would look unthreatened and similar, the Alfonsín government would appear embattled in sustained conflict, and Uruguay would be located between these two extremes. However, when we include the dimension of prerogatives we get a more complex, accurate, and dynamic sense of civil-military relations in the four democratizing countries. These prerogatives are the subject of the next chapter.

[29] For a discussion of the multiple coup movements in early 1981, see Carolyn P. Boyd and James Boyden, "The Armed Forces and the Transition to Democracy in Spain."

# CHAPTER 7

# The Military in Newly
# Democratic Regimes: The Dimension
# of Military Prerogatives

ANALYTICALLY DISTINCT, though obviously connected to the issue of articulated conflict, is the matter of military prerogatives. The Oxford English Dictionary defines a prerogative as "a prior, exclusive, or peculiar right or privilege," and, as "a faculty or property by which a being is specially and advantageously distinguished above others." For our purposes, the dimension of military institutional prerogatives refers to those areas where, whether challenged or not, the military as an institution assumes they have an acquired right or privilege, formal or informal, to exercise effective control over its internal governance, to play a role within extramilitary areas within the state apparatus, or even to structure relationships between the state and political or civil society. Table 7.1 presents some of the most important potential military prerogatives, and indicates what would constitute "low," "moderate," and "high" prerogatives. Note that when the military is classified as having a "low" prerogative it is because de jure and de facto effective control over the prerogative is exercised by the officials, procedures and institutions sanctioned by the democratic regime. In cases where the military has de jure been denied a prerogative, but the new democratic government, due to active or passive noncompliance by the military, does not effectively exercise this prerogative, military prerogatives would not be classified as "low" but as "moderate."

Empirically every military prerogative can be contested. If the military strongly resists an attempt by a new democratic government to reduce military prerogatives such military resistance would be reflected in the conflict dimension. Analytically, however, it is useful to distinguish between the conflict dimension and

TABLE 7.1. Selected Prerogatives of Military as Institution in a Democratic Regime

| | Low | Moderate | High |
|---|---|---|---|
| 1. Constitutionally sanctioned independent role of the military in political system: | None. Military actions to bolster internal security are only undertaken when ordered by the appropriate executive official within a framework established by legal system and the legislature. | | Constitution allocates primary responsibility for internal law and order to the military and implicitly gives military great decisional latitude in determining when and how to carry out their responsibilities. |
| 2. Military relationship to the chief executive: | Chief executive (president, prime minister, or constitutional monarch) is de jure and de facto commander-in-chief. | | De facto control of the armed forces is in the hands of the uniformed active-duty service commanders. |
| 3. Coordination of defense sector: | De jure and de facto, done by Cabinet-level official (normally a civilian appointed by chief executive) who controls a staff with extensive participation by professional civil servants or civilian political appointees. | | De jure and de facto, done by service chiefs separately, with very weak or nonexistent supervision by Joint General Staff and with weak comprehensive planning by chief executive. |

| | | | |
|---|---|---|---|
| 4. Active-duty military participation in the Cabinet: | Normally none. | Active-duty commanders of each service also serve in Cabinet as ministers of their service. | Three active-duty military ministers plus a variety of other ministers, especially those with national security tasks (intelligence, National Security Council, etc.). |
| 5. Role of legislature: | Most major policy issues affecting military budgets, force structure, and new weapons initiatives are monitored by the legislature. Cabinet-level officials and chief aides routinely appear before legislative committees to defend and explain policy initiatives and to present legislation. | | Legislature simply approves or disapproves executive's budget. No legislative tradition of detailed hearings on defense matters. Military seldom if ever provides legislature with detailed information about defense sector, and top officials of the defense sector seldom if ever appear at legislative committee meetings. |
| 6. Role of senior career civil servants or civilian political appointees: | Professional cadre of highly informed civil servants or policy-making civilian political appointees play a major role in assisting executive branch in designing and implementing defense and national security policy. | | Active-duty military officials fill almost all top defense sector staff roles. Civilian participants normally do so as employees of the three military services. |

TABLE 7.1. (*continued*)

|  | Low | Moderate | High |
|---|---|---|---|
| 7. Role in intelligence: | Peak intelligence agencies *de jure* and *de facto* controlled by civilian chains of command. Strong civilian review boards. |  | Peak intelligence agencies controlled by active-duty, general-level officers who combine intelligence gathering and operations functions. No independent review boards. |
| 8. Role in police: | Police under control of nonmilitary ministry or local officials. No active-duty military allowed to command a police unit. | Police under control of non-military ministry or local officials. Active-duty military officers allowed to serve in police. | Police under overall direct command of military and most local police chiefs are active-duty military. |
| 9. Role in military promotions: | Legislature has discussed and approved promotion law. Professional military promotion board makes recommendation to Cabinet-level officials who in turn make recommendations to executive. Executive not typically constrained in selection of major policy-making posts. |  | Military has played a major role in setting the boundaries for promotion patterns. Executive very tightly constrained in who can be chosen from promotions list forwarded by each service. |

| | | | |
|---|---|---|---|
| 10. Role in state enterprises: | Only exceptionally does an active-duty military officer head a state enterprise. | Military reserve officers routinely found in high positions in state enterprises, but normally no active-duty officers would head a state enterprise. | Occasionally by law and normally by tradition, active-duty military officers control key state enterprises. |
| 11. Role in legal system: | Military have almost no legal jurisdiction outside of narrowly defined internal offenses against military discipline. In all areas outside this domain, civilians and military are subject to civil laws and civil courts. | | National-security laws and military-court system cover large areas of political and civil society. Domain where military can be tried in civil courts is very narrow. |

the prerogative dimension because a number of quite different relationships are possible between the two dimensions within a democracy. In an uncontested model of civilian control of the military, both military prerogatives and articulated conflict are low.

It is conceivable that the military could go from a position of high prerogatives to relatively low prerogatives without contestation. Empirically such an absence of military contestation would be most likely to occur within the overall context of a sociopolitical situation that approximates what I have elsewhere labeled as the "restoration" path of redemocratization.[1] In such a path the military might accept a reduction of their prerogatives without contestation if such a pattern of low prerogatives were seen as an integral part, by both the military and the civilian leaders, of the overall model of governance and of civil-military relations that is being restored.

It is also possible, however, to have a situation in which there is low articulated conflict but there are high military prerogatives. High military prerogatives can exist even if not challenged by the top political leaders of the new democratic regime. The power asymmetry between the military and the new regime may be such that there is never an open contestation over clear policy alternatives; a range of potential issues becomes "nonissues"; and the new democratic politicians may "accommodate" themselves to this reality for a variety of reasons.

The dimension of articulated conflict discussed in the previous chapter involves the kind of open contestation integral to Robert Dahl's conceptualization of power and is a very important dimension of civil-military relations. However, since military power can derive from a series of prerogatives that it has acquired ideologically or politically, we must recognize these prerogatives as a form of latent independent structural power within the polity even in cases where there is almost no articulated conflict.[2]

[1] See my "Paths Toward Redemocratization: Theoretical and Comparative Considerations," 64–67.

[2] The major form of power that Robert Dahl evaluates in his classic, *Who Governs?*, is that revealed in open contestation. For a discussion of the debate about other forms of power, see Steven Lukes, *Power: A Radical View*.

Analytically it is important to recognize the independent existence of the conflict dimension and the prerogative dimension. However, we gain analytic power when we combine both dimensions of civil-military control, as shown in Figure 7.1.

If we bound our two dimensions as in Figure 7.2, and call everything within this "property space" democratic (although some positions are straining toward breakdown), we arrive at four possible extreme coordinates of civil-military relations within a democracy.[3]

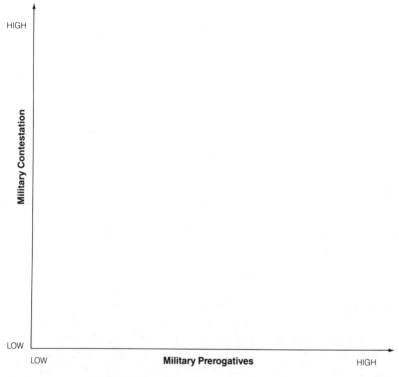

Figure 7.1 Two dimensions of civil-military control.

[3] The concept of "property space" was originally formulated by Paul Lazarsfeld. For discussion and application of the concept, see *The Language of Social*

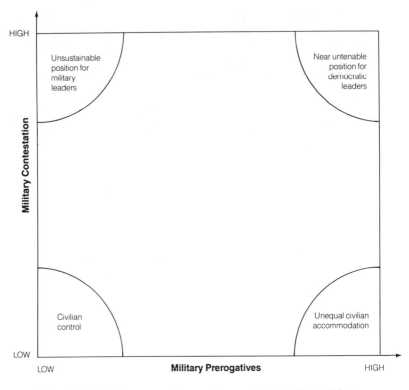

Figure 7.2 Contestation, prerogatives, and democratic civil-military relations.

The bottom left-hand corner where low civil-military contestation and low military prerogatives come together can be called "civilian control." To say that this position represents "civilian control" does not mean that developments might not emerge which could ultimately upset civilian control and threaten democracy. The relationships possible within Figure 7.2 are not static but subject to a constant play of forces and are thus inherently dynamic. No democracy in the world should be seen as theoreti-

*Research*, ed. Paul Lazarsfeld and Morris Rosenberg, 40–62. For the manner of visually depicting my argument in Figure 7.2, I am indebted to Robert A. Dahl, *Polyarchy*, 6–7.

cally or empirically immune to crises that might eventually upset even a once-consolidated model of civilian control. However, to say that civilian control exists is by no means a trivial assertion. It is to say that the existing model itself—as recognized by both the military and democratic leaders—does not present independent sources of instability to the functioning of democracy.

The bottom right-hand corner, low military contestation and high military prerogatives, can be called "unequal civilian accommodation." From the perspective of democratic theory, a polity in this position has important vulnerabilities because of the military's latent structural powers entailed in their possession of so many prerogatives. One serious vulnerability is that the policy process might become quite conflictual, and the military, backed by weighty allies in civil and political society, might utilize all their prerogatives to urge a series of policy outcomes that the leaders of the democratic regime accept to avoid a coup. The outcome of this "white coup" would be a nondemocratic system.

Another vulnerability of the "unequal civilian accommodation" position is that a polity could become transformed into a nondemocratic civilian-headed garrison state because of exploitation by the executive of the prerogatives the military retained in the system. An additional basic weakness of this position is that the lack of regime autonomy from the military implied in such high military prerogatives could delegitimize the new democracy in the eyes of civil and even political society.

Inherent in a pattern of "unequal civilian accommodation" is that at some future time the electoral process could produce a chief executive and a legislature who are given a mandate to impose a variety of reforms that would challenge military prerogatives. The civilians might triumph, in which case civilian-military relations would no longer be characterized as "unequal civilian accommodation." However, the democratic reform government's attempt to reduce military prerogatives might generate sharp military resistance in which the military prevails in the crises. This would mean that civil-military relations would lead to a high conflict–high prerogatives situation as found in the upper right-hand corner of Figure 7.2.

No matter how the political system arrives at the high conflict–high prerogatives position, it is one that is fraught with dangers for democratic consolidation. Depending on the balance of power, it will lead to a breakdown of democracy or, after a sustained struggle, to the democratic government constructing a civil-military alliance that reduces prerogatives and reduces conflict.

The fourth extreme position is one of low military prerogatives and high conflict. This position in its purest sense is analytically possible but empirically unlikely, especially if we remember that "low" military prerogatives implies *de facto* as well as *de jure* civilian control. If such a low prerogative–high conflict position were reached, it would probably have occurred relatively quickly, and the civilian government would be in a reasonably good power position to defuse the conflict by changing military leaders.

Historically, situations that analysts might think are ones of low military prerogatives and high conflict are probably on closer inspection situations that—like Chile from 1970 to 1973—started near the lower left-hand corner and ones in which over time, owing to conflicts in the political system, the military either were given or acquired prerogatives they had previously not had.[4]

Within the context of our two dimensions, any position in the property space presented in Figure 7.2 is possible for a democratic regime. Our ability to address the question of where a new democratic regime is located in the figure helps us to recognize what types of civil-military problems the regime initially faces. The figure could also give practitioners a map of existing power relationships which they could use when they design a strategy aimed at empowering themselves to increase their capacity to manage civil-military relations democratically. Finally, the figure enables us to chart change, or to note the absence of change, over time.

---

[4] See Arturo Valenzuela, *The Breakdown of Democratic Regimes: Chile*, esp. 20–21, 81–110. The Chilean military were probably never fully in the bottom left-hand corner, however, in that even in 1967, 84 percent of the retired generals held the opinion in a poll that the military should act as "a guardian of the constitution in case a government tries to violate it." See Roy Allen Hansen, "Military Culture and Organizational Decline: A Study of the Chilean Army," 254.

MILITARY PREROGATIVES IN BRAZIL

The country where our understanding of the deep structure of civil-military relations is most altered when we consider prerogatives is Brazil. In terms of the eleven prerogatives presented in Table 7.1, the Brazilian military acquired prerogatives when they ended the empire in 1889, these increased during the Vargas dictatorship, especially during the Estado Novo of 1937–1945. Even though the constitution was rewritten in 1946, the military retained many of these prerogatives.[5] In Brazil, a weak party system has historically coexisted with extreme social inequality, and the drafters of Brazilian constitutions, ever since the Republic was founded in 1889, have accorded the military a significant role in the maintenance of internal order. For these reasons, the military during the last period of civilian rule (1946–1964) enjoyed high prerogatives concerning their role in the constitution, the coordination of the defense sector, their role in the cabinet, and their control over civilians who were involved in defense policies (variables 1, 3, 4, and 6). In this period the military also exercised no less than moderate prerogatives for all seven remaining variables.

During the most intense period of repressive military rule (1969–1972), military prerogatives were high, or close to high, on all eleven variables. During the Geisel government, military prerogatives vis-à-vis the chief executive and promotions (variables 2 and 9) were reduced from high to moderate. However, in the first two years of civilian rule the only possible new areas where military prerogatives were reduced concerned the police and state enterprises (variables 8 and 10), where their *de facto*, but not *de jure*, prerogatives were reduced slightly. However, *de facto* military control over promotions has returned to high. President Geisel

---

[5] Part of the explanation may have been because the military overthrew Vargas in 1945 and thus claimed authorship of the new democracy. In addition, the two major presidential candidates in the 1945 direct elections were general-level officers. The victor, General Dutra, had been a Minister of War and a key figure in the Estado Novo. Elite reluctance to curtail military prerogatives may have been reinforced in 1946 because the constitution was written in a period of intense social mobilization. For an account of the atmosphere in which the 1946 Constitution was written, see Peter Flynn, *Brazil: A Political Analysis*, 110–140.

altered promotion lists, President Figuereido prenegotiated them, but President Sarnay, by most accounts, simply ratified all nominations without discussion. Thus in the first two years of the present civilian government, the Brazilian military has been able to retain significant control over much of the political space they had occupied during the twenty-one years of military rule.

The question of military prerogatives deserves a full-scale study. For our purposes, however, let me just analyze a few of these prerogatives in detail, making a particular effort to explore how they contribute to latent military power in the polity, and giving concrete examples of how this latent power has on occasion been tellingly brought to bear in the first two years of civilian rule.

The first prerogative to pay attention to is military participation in the Cabinet. Since the mid-1920s, all service heads have always served in the Cabinet with full ministerial status. Uniformed general-grade officers thus serve as the Minister of the Army, Minister of the Navy, and Minister of the Air Force. During the military government of 1964–1985, two additional positions that are ex officio held by a general-level officer were accorded ministerial status, the chief of the Military Cabinet (who is also secretary-general of the National Security Council) and the chief of the Armed Forces General Staff (EMFA). Finally, during the military government, as we documented earlier, the Serviço Nacional de Informações was created as the country's peak domestic and international intelligence agency, and the chief was given ministerial rank. Since 1969 the directorship of the SNI, although it can by law be held by a civilian, has always been occupied by an active-duty army general. In sum, before and after democratization the Brazilian cabinet contained six active-duty general-grade officers.

Does it matter? Does it involve the military ministers in general political issues? On the day that Congress reopened the March 1986 session, the Minister of the Army, General Leônidas Pires Gonçalves, addressed the question in no uncertain terms:

> I am a military man, but I have a political aspect [*faceta*] and it is my right to express this aspect. I will use it with parsimony but it is a right which I will not yield. I consider it unjust for

anyone to deny me this right. I am a soldier, but I am a Minister; Ministers have political aspects and I think I have the right to say some things about political issues. . . . I am very concerned about this country.[6]

Actually, he and the other five military ministers routinely and forcefully either supported publicly, or advocated effectively within government councils, strong positions on most of the major issues on the Brazilian political agenda.[7]

Most modern democracies and modern military organizations now have a Cabinet-level civilian who coordinates the defense sector. In Brazil there has never been a Minister of Defense. After 1985 the proposal was aired from time to time that a civilian should be made Minister of Defense and the service heads of the army, navy, air force, and the chief of the armed forces General Staff lose their ministerial status. However, the persistent response of the military was that the proposal was simply premature and should not be seriously considered at this time—and it was not.[8] The military opposition has virtually reduced this potentially explosive issue to a nonissue.

To a significant extent this means that the three services have a high degree of autonomy in the development of their plans vis-à-

[6] "Leônidas Defende Direito de Falar," *O Estado de S. Paulo*, March 2, 1986.

[7] See, for example, "Leônidas Condena as Diretas Já," *O Estado de S. Paulo*, December 18, 1985, and "O General Não Admite Redução do Mandato," *Jornal da Tarde*, February 28, 1986. The Constituent Assembly's deliberations about the possible adoption of a parliamentary form of government were also strongly influenced by the military. The three service heads and the Minister of the Military Household expressed a strong desire to maintain direct access to the president and not to be subject, as the prime minister and almost all the other ministers would be, to a congressional vote of no confidence. If some variant of this parliamentary formula prevails, it will yield a more extreme version of a dual executive than that found in any existing parliamentary system in the world, including that of France.

[8] See "Um Civil no Ministério da Defesa?" *Jornal da Tarde*, June 5, 1986. The members of the preliminary constitutional drafting commission were reported to have been early advocates of a Ministry of Defense and a national police force, but to have withdrawn these proposals when they saw they had no backing from the military ministers. See "Militares Não Admitem Ter Funções Reduzidas," *O Estado de S. Paulo*, June 6, 1986.

vis the chief executive. Their autonomy is compounded by the fact that traditionally the Brazilian legislature does not have regular committee meetings with ministers, especially military ministers. The Brazilian legislature has virtually no routine ways to ask and receive detailed documentation about major defense initiatives. Neither the announcement of the major modernization plans of the armed forces in 1985, nor the discovery in August 1986 of a probable nuclear test site, yielded any congressional involvement in fact-finding or monitoring.

The absence of a civilian-controlled Ministry of Defense, and the virtual nonparticipation of Congress and parties in routine analysis of defense issues, means that at the level of the state, and even of political society, there are almost no civilian specialists on military affairs who are not direct employees of a military-led ministry. The successful retention by the military of their prerogatives in this area has directly sustained their comparative mastery vis-à-vis civilians over both strategic and technical defense issues. This makes the creation of an effective model of civilian control difficult.

Two military-controlled posts that entail the procedural right, and the range of resources, to influence not only the operations of the state but numerous aspects of political and civil society are the chief of the Serviço Nacional de Informações, and the secretary-general of the National Security Council. By tradition these two positions are deeply involved in most conflictual issues facing the Brazilian polity, and have some superministerial prerogatives.

Are prerogatives power? Yes, if the exercise of these prerogatives helps to turn potential issues on the political agenda into nonissues, if their exercise sets boundaries to political conflict in the polity, if their existence facilitates the appeal to their exercise by civilians who have interests to protect and thus want the military to remain strong players in the political system, or if the strong defense of the prerogatives prevents major political initiatives from being implemented once they have begun. All these elements of power were in fact quite present and visible in the first two years of civilian rule.

Let me illustrate how military prerogatives have had a significant impact on five of the most important policy issues the civilian government faced in the first two years of its existence. One issue area concerned how the past would be addressed, three involved major policies of the present, and one involved a critical decision for the future.

The area that concerned the past was how to treat human-rights offenders who continued to hold positions in the state apparatus. Because of the amnesty of 1979, which covered all crimes up to that date, trials for pre-1979 offenses, as we saw in Chapter 6, were not an issue of deep contestation. However, it was widely hoped that the new democratic regime would, where possible, remove known torturers from important positions. The first clear test concerning this issue occurred when a congresswoman, Bete Mendes, informed President Sarney that when she was on an official mission to Uruguay she encountered an officer involved in her torture, a Colonel Ustra, who was then a Brazilian army attaché in Uruguay. President Sarney responded by apparently ordering a change in post for the attaché. The Minister of the Army, General Leônidas, exercising what he apparently viewed as his prerogative to control army posting, in essence challenged the order by issuing the following statement to the Army:

> Colonel Ustra is our army attaché in Uruguay. He enjoys our confidence and will remain there until he completes his normal tour. Those who acted patriotically against the subversives and the terrorists, pardoned by the amnesty, merit the respect of our institution for the success they achieved, often at the risk of their own life.[9]

The minister's forceful advocacy contributed not only to the predominance of the military in this particular case of conflict over prerogatives, but comparable acts of active or passive noncompliance by top military officers contributed to an atmosphere in which, during the first two years of civilian government, not one

---

[9] "Leônidas Mantém Adido no Uruguai," *O Estado de S. Paulo*, August 24, 1985, and "A Contra-Ordem do Ministro do Exército," *Jornal da Tarde*, August 27, 1985. *Veja*, Brazil's most influential weekly, later said Ustra "commanded the most ferocious torture center of the regime," March 18, 1987, 28.

conviction for terrorism committed by security forces after 1979 was handed down by any court.

Three of the most important new policy issues that emerged in the first two years of civilian government concerned how the government should proceed with agrarian reform, how Brazil could transcend its corporatist pattern of labor relations concerning strikes, and whether Brazil could make progress on its bold scheme for market integration with the newly democratic countries of Argentina and Uruguay. In all three of these new initiatives, military officers utilizing prerogatives they enjoyed within the state apparatus played critical boundary-setting roles.

The announcement by President Sarney of an agrarian reform plan sent the Brazilian countryside into a turmoil of peasant action and landowner counteraction. General Bayma Denys, the secretary-general of the National Security Council, who had previously defended a broad interpretation of his prerogatives by asserting that ''all the issues of various domains of power are followed, because from one hour to the next they can be transformed into security issues,'' soon issued an extensive interministerial plan on how the government should proceed in agrarian reform.[10]

In May 1986 President Sarney approved agrarian reform plans for eighteen regions and said he would help ensure peaceful change by the use of the military.[11] Soon thereafter a retired colonel was placed in charge of INCRA, the main agency responsible for agrarian reform. When his minister objected to the colonel's policy orientation, he was told by the chief of the SNI that the president wanted the minister's resignation.[12] In June it was announced that military engineering units would be present in areas of agrarian reform.[13] In July the SNI, whose top officials are active-

[10] For three informative articles about the role of General Denys see ''General Denys Mostra a Nova Segurança Nacional,'' *Folha da Tarde*, April 20, 1985; ''Decisão Foi Baseada em Documento de Bayma Denys,'' *Folha de S. Paulo*, September 28, 1985; and ''Denys Representa no Planalto a Face Dura do Velho Sistema,'' *Jornal do Brasil*, September 29, 1985.

[11] ''Sarney: Exército Pode Garantir os Planos,'' *Jornal da Tarde*, May 19, 1986.

[12] ''Ex-Ministro Ainda Queria Ficar,'' *Jornal do Brasil*, May 29, 1986.

[13] ''Exército Presente em Areas de Conflito,'' *O Estado de S. Paulo*, June 3, 1986.

duty army officers, released a report prepared for President Sarney in which they argued that "leftist infiltration" was serious in the agrarian reform agency and that forty-one of the top eighty-seven agency leaders had leftist backgrounds. Shortly thereafter it was announced that thirteen of the officials no longer worked for the agency and two more would soon leave.[14] The period of major change in agrarian reform seemed to be over. In the first major domestic reform of the New Republic, the agrarian reform, the military played an important role in monitoring, boundary setting, and implementation.

We should be careful nonetheless as to how we interpret the role of the military in agrarian reform. Numerous influential groups in civil and political society, and within the state apparatus, were opposed to agrarian reform, and the most active use of force involved not the military but gun-men hired by landowners. Some were opposed because their material interests were threatened; others were opposed because they feared a general radicalization of the Brazilian countryside. Most of these groups directly or indirectly were supporters of military involvement in regulating the process. Here the issue of civil-military alliances is crucial. Civilian groups who want the military to retain power resources to which they can appeal not only do not challenge these resources, but they oppose any initiatives to reduce military prerogatives. The military was not only a passive instrument, however. The exercise of their prerogatives in this area helped contain the political conflict the military feared, and helped to demonstrate to powerful groups in civil society that the military had potentially useful political resources that should not be challenged.[15]

One of the most potentially fruitful initiatives in recent Latin American history was the effort by the presidents of the newly democratizing governments of Brazil and Argentina in 1986 to create an incipient common market between the two countries. Extensive co-development of advanced technology, including nu-

[14] "Dossiê do SNI Aponta 'Infiltração Esquerdista' no INCRA," *Folha de S. Paulo*, July 17, 1986.

[15] For a discussion of the complex sociopolitical coalition to slow agrarian reform, see Ricardo Abramovay, "O Velho Poder dos Barões da Terra."

clear technology, was to be an integral part of the initiatives. However, it increasingly became clear, in a variety of forums, that the Brazilian military had grave reservations about the codevelopment of high technology with Argentina because such codevelopment could affect adversely Brazil's strategic autonomy. Opposition was strongest in those areas involving the Brazilian military's three distinct nuclear projects, where neither the executive nor legislative branches of the New Republic have yet demonstrated any capacity to monitor or alter military plans. The integration initiative continues, but its content has been unilaterally narrowed by military action.[16]

Another major issue area was that of strikes. The chief government official in charge of handling strikes and creating new procedures to dismantle slowly the corporatist tradition of labor relations was the Minister of Labor, Almir Pazzianotto. However, when a bank workers' strike in September 1985 put the new labor system to its first major test, Pazzianotto repeatedly found his space for negotiation reduced by initiatives taken by General Ivan de Souza Mendes, chief of the SNI; General Denys, the secretary-general of the National Security Council; and the military police.[17]

The role of the army in strikes was clearest during the effort by labor in December 1986 to launch Brazil's first general strike since 1917. The army, in the exercise of its prerogative to maintain internal law and order and equipped with armored personnel carriers and automatic weapons, occupied Volta Redonda, Brazil's main steel mill, surprised the governor of São Paulo by occupying a federal steel mill located in São Paulo, and conspicuously assumed control of the railroad station and numerous key thorough-

[16] This analysis is based on discussions in Brazil with military and political leaders in August 1986, and in February and June 1987. In the first eighteen months of the accord, the only concrete plan agreed upon with any military dimension was for the extremely modest codevelopment of a nineteen-seat short-hop airplane whose predominant buyers will be commercial airlines. See "Brasil e Argentina já Planejam o Novo Avião," *O Estado de S. Paulo*, May 22, 1987.

[17] For a detailed account of government policy making during the strike, which includes an assertion that the ministers who "talked most" at the critical Cabinet meeting were General de Souza Mendes and General Denys, see "A Greve dos Bancários Falou Grosso," *Veja*, September 18, 1985, 36–43.

fares in Rio de Janeiro.[18]Two questions emerge when this heavy involvement of the army in strikes is analyzed. Why was the army used almost as the first resort, not, as in most functioning democracies, as the last resort? And who authorized the deployment of regular army troops?[19] This leads us to the basic questions of the constitutional role of the military in the polity, the chain of command for issues that concern the maintenance of internal order, and military perceptions of their own just roles. What do the military *believe* their prerogatives *should be* within the political system as a whole? This is a fundamental question for a modern democracy. Robert Dahl has succinctly stated the issue:

Where the military is relatively large, centralized, and hierarchial, as it is in most countries today, polyarchy is of course impossible unless the military is sufficiently depolitized to permit civilian rule. . . . The crucial intervening factor, clearly, is one of beliefs. . . . The point to be made here is simple and obvious: the chances for polyarchy today are directly dependent on the strength of certain beliefs not only among civilian but among all ranks of the military.[20]

In Brazil, do the military accept that the president, subject to appropriate legislative approval, is the sole legitimate source of commands concerning the use of military force? Or do they be-

[18] See "Exército no Rio, Piquetes em B.H.," and "No Rio, Exército Ocupa a Estação Ferroviaria," both articles in *O Estado de S. Paulo*, December 12, 1986.

[19] In March 1987 the army and navy were sent even more massively to protect oil refineries and ports from strikes. President Sarney was the overall author of these troop movements, but many of the decisions about timing and use had a high military component. The Minister of the Navy, for example, assumed full responsibility for giving the order to send marines to take control of the ports: "There was no necessity for the President to consult with ministers or the National Security Council. I myself took the decision as soon as I heard that the Judiciary considered the strike illegal." The civilian Minister of Labor said he was not consulted or asked to play any mediating role and was only informed after troops and tanks were moving. See *Veja* cover story, March 18, 1987, 23.

[20] Robert A. Dahl, *Polyarchy*, 50.

lieve they have a right to discretionary obedience and the right to take major initiatives in the area of domestic order?

Their attitudes toward this critical question became apparent in their remarks concerning what should, and what should not, be altered in the Brazilian constitution. The issue was on the Brazilian agenda because a Constituent Assembly was elected in November 1986 and began deliberations in February 1987.

The previous constituent assemblies of 1891, 1934, and 1946 all wrote into the Brazilian constitution two critical clauses specifically relevant to the civil-military model. One clause stated that the military should obey the president "within the limits of the law." The other clause stated that the military was a permanent national institution which was specifically charged with the task of maintaining internal law and order in the country and of guaranteeing the normal functioning of the three constitutional powers. In a previous study I discussed these clauses at length. I argued that the "within the limits of the law" clause had the danger of legitimizing discretionary obedience and thus fostering a deliberative role for the military. Likewise, the internal law-and-order maintenance clause provided language that facilitated military involvement in the adjudication and structuring of domestic conflict. Interestingly, in all three previous constituent assembly debates these critical clauses were introduced by civilians who either wanted to be able to check the president or to have the military available as an instrument of domestic dispute containment. In the three previous constituent assembly debates, the military had not championed these clauses because they feared divisive involvement in politics.[21]

After twenty-one years of military government between 1964 and 1985, the terms of the debate changed. Unlike in 1891, 1934, or 1946, the military, especially the army, now clearly wanted these constitutional prerogatives. The military ministers, their official representative in the commission set up to study the consti-

---

[21] See Stepan, *The Military in Politics*, Chapters 4 and 5. See esp. 74–79, which discuss the constituent-assembly debates and the military clauses. Pages 99–115 analyze how the constitution was actually utilized by civilian and military alike to argue for and to legitimate actual military intervention.

tution, and the military lobby in Congress launched an extensive campaign to win allies and neutralize opponents.

In the first few months of civilian rule, most military statements simply affirmed that the existing constitutional clauses should be maintained. For example, the Minister of the Navy said that "the present constitutional attributions [concerning the Armed Forces] are perfect. Nothing should be changed."[22] In June 1986 a first draft was released by the Provisional Commission on Constitutional Studies. It eliminated the "within the limits of the law" clause, and explicitly said the military mission was external and that "the maintenance of public order . . . is the duty of the civil police which are subordinated to the Executive power" of the states of the federation. The states were also given the right to set up and supervise military police.

The draft indicated that in extreme cases of disorder the president could declare a state of siege; but he would immediately have to give his reason for doing so to the Congress, which would have the right to ratify or revoke the state of siege. Under conditions where the president and the Congress had authorized a state of siege, the president could place the state police under military command.[23]

Following publication of the draft constitutional project, the papers in Brazil were filled with hostile military reactions. The critical issue at stake was: Who was to decide *when*, *if*, and *how* the military might be used in domestic affairs. Again and again the subtext of the army position was that the issue should be left vague enough so that, if necessary, the military, by themselves, could make the decision while not being in violation of the constitution.[24]

---

[22] Quoted in *O Estado de S. Paulo*, June 12, 1985.

[23] The twenty-one articles concerning the military and national security provisions of the Comissão Provisória de Estudos Constitucionais are printed in full in "Comissão Altera Função das Forças Armadas," *O Estado de S. Paulo*, June 5, 1986.

[24] For numerous quotes from high active-duty military officers where this emerges as the central issue, see "Um Civil no Ministério da Defesa?" *Jornal da Tarde*, June 5, 1986; "A Reação (enérgica) dos Generais," *Jornal da Tarde*, Jan-

A later version of the draft commission report gave the military significant leeway in internal affairs, and some commission members openly acknowledged that they had been influenced by the great clamor raised by the military.[25] By January 1987 the ideological climate and civil-military power relations in the country were such that more than half the members of the constituent assembly said that they were in favor of some internal defense role for the military. Both President Sarney and a major candidate for his job, Ulysses Guimarães, the president of the Constituent Assembly and a longtime critic of excessive involvement of the military in politics, were advocates of the retention of the traditional constitutional role of the military in domestic affairs.[26]

## MILITARY PREROGATIVES IN ARGENTINA

Argentina is like Brazil in one important respect. Since the 1930's the military has enjoyed a reasonably high degree of autonomy concerning some of its key prerogatives within the state apparatus.

President Alfonsín is thus attempting to eliminate prerogatives and impinge on degrees of autonomy that in many cases have existed for more than half a century. Since civilian politicians and

---

uary 5, 1986; "Militares Não Admitem Ter Funções Reduzidas," *O Estado de S. Paulo*, June 6, 1986; and "Os Militares Não Querem Mudar de Papel," *Jornal da Tarde*, September 2, 1986.

The most forceful statement concerning the military prerogative to decide when and how military force should be employed in domestic conflicts was that attributed to the Minister of the Army in an interview. On the Day of the Soldier he was quoted as saying that the armed forces "aspire to maintain untouched their privilege to interfere in the destiny of the Republic whenever they judge that the constitutional powers, law, and order are in danger." I attach, analytically, somewhat less significance to this quote than to the others I have referred to because, even if the minister was quoted correctly, it is an extreme statement that was not repeated in such bold terms again. See "O Constituinte Fardado," *Senhor*, January 29, 1987, 93.

[25] For a discussion of how and why the drafting commission reversed itself, see "Comissão Dá a Militares Atribução de Garantir 'Ordem Constitucional'," *Folha de S. Paulo*, September 1, 1986, and "Arinos Quer Rever Decisão Sobre Forças Armadas," *Folha de S. Paulo*, July 11, 1986.

[26] See "Defesa da Ordem," *Veja*, February 4, 1987, 24.

specialists have not really occupied the commanding heights of civil-miltary relations in the last half-century, part of Alfonsín's task is to create civilian capacities, institutions, and attitudes conducive to the exercise of power.

As we have seen in our previous discussion, President Alfonsín formally reduced some of the Argentine military's important prerogatives. His government now certainly has greater control over the military budget, promotions, and military industries. It has also challenged military claims concerning the autonomy of the military court system and sentenced key leaders of the previous military regime for human-rights abuses. However, it is also true to say that virtually every prerogative that has been formally taken away is the subject of contestation. There is a Minister of Defense, but he is having great difficulty doing comprehensive planning. The peak intelligence systems are now in civilian hands but the army intelligence units, especially the 602 Battalion, have extensive formal and especially informal power capabilities. Most ominously, the hasty government move in December 1986 to have a *punto final* to the trials was in response to the growing resistance of younger active-duty officers against any trials of active-duty officers. At the start of his fourth year of government, Alfonsín was facing a military that had not fully reconciled themselves to the loss of their prerogatives, and which were beginning to recompose themselves after their post-Malvinas disarray. On the civilian side, many of the prerogatives the civilians have claimed as theirs still await the composition of a coherent corpus of qualified civilians who will implement—in the areas of the Defense Ministry and the legislature—the new model of civil-miltary relations President Alfonsín has articulated.

In Argentina, after three years of civilian democratic rule, the old model of civil-military relations had been severely challenged. Almost all the formal military prerogatives had been removed. However, the legitimacy and efficacy of the proposed new model remained deeply questioned by the military, as the events surrounding the 1987 Easter week junior-officer mutinies revealed. The intensity of the conflict was illustrated by four key aspects of the Easter week crisis. First, Alfonsín received extraordinary support from both civil society and the major parties of political society. Second, despite the declared intention of various generals that they would support Alfonsín, no general was actually able to deliver "a rifle" to repress the mutinies. Third, in the aftermath of the mutinies, most generals felt that the army's hierarchy had been completely broken. Fourth, Alfonsín, faced with a deteriorating military situation, rushed through a much more extensive "due obedience" amnesty than previously planned.[27]

## MILITARY PREROGATIVES IN URUGUAY

The situation in Uruguay is remarkably different from that of Brazil or Argentina. A strong hypothesis could be made that the Uruguayan transition to a great extent is seen both by the military and by the new government as a case of *restoration* of the *status quo ante* in civilian-military relations. That is, the civil-military model that prevailed before the crises of the late 1960s led to the installation of a bureacratic-authoritarian regime in 1973 is seen as an appropriate model. Military acceptance of the old model may have been facilitated by the fact that when in the 1980 plebiscite they made an effort to institutionalize a new model—which gave them greatly enhanced prerogatives—no significant sector of political or civil society supported them, and they were soundly defeated.[28]

The restoration of traditional civilian prerogatives and the pat-

[27] The above assessment is based on interviews with a military liaison officer to Congress, with a ranking senator, with a ranking deputy, and with some staff members of the congressional defense commissions, as well as various advisers to Alfonsín, in Buenos Aires, May 22–23, 1987, and in New York.

For a detailed and careful analysis of civil-military relations in Argentina, see Andrés Fontana, "De la Crisis de Malvinas a la Subordinación Condicionada: Conflictos Intramilitares y Transición Política en Argentina." Also see Virgilio R. Beltrám, "Political Transition in Argentina: 1982 to 1985." For the "due obedience" law, see Shirley Christian, "Argentina Seeks to Limit Abuse Charges," *The New York Times*, May 14, 1987.

[28] In this context, see Alfred Stepan, "State Power and Civil Society in the Southern Cone," 325–329. Internal splits and political and economic problems in the last four years of military rule reinforced the perception of the basic illegitimacy of the military as a political actor, even in the eyes of military leaders.

terns of behavior associated with this model have not led to intense articulated conflict. Uruguay's long history as a democracy, especially a democracy in which the legislature had important powers, had created a climate in Uruguay, more than in Argentina or Brazil, where the military accepted as normal a relatively narrow scope of prerogatives, and civilians actively sought to reestablish the norm that they should manage military affairs. The importance of this prior culture was evident in the underlying tone of my interviews. The tone was startlingly different from the one I encountered in Brazil. For example, in Uruguay both civilian leaders and military leaders stressed that it would be "completely incorrect" and not in accordance with military law for active-duty generals to serve in state agencies; that "of course" the Senate asks for, and receives, detailed information on weapons purchases; and that "obviously" the Minister of Defense appeared before Congress as a matter of "routine."

Consistent with this political culture in Uruguay, in the early months of the new government a general who complained vociferously about a key appointment in the Ministry of Defense and a general who complained about military budgets were summarily sacked without serious repercussions because their behavior violated the norm. Also, the military has not been seen on the streets during any strikes because as both military and government officials stress, monitoring of strikes is a police function.

Uruguay until the mid-1960s was a system in which the military prerogatives would have approximated the low end of Table 7.1. During the bureaucratic-authoritarian regime, the military wanted to rule collectively via the Junta de Generales composed of all four-star officers in the army, navy, and air force. In this period their military prerogatives were higher than in Brazil. In the Pacto del Club Naval the military demanded and received a series of one-year limitations on the incoming civilian government as the price of military extrication.[29] President Sanguinetti adhered to the constraints of the Pacto del Club Naval. However, after the

---

[29] See Juan Rial, "Las Fuerzas Armadas: Soldados-políticos Garantes de la Democracia?"

agreed-upon transitional year had passed, he gradually reassumed what he asserted were the president's traditional prerogatives vis-à-vis the military. The military, in turn, with the extremely important exception of the military trials where they refused to appear physically before civilian courts, have without major contestation reverted to the *status quo ante* concerning their prerogatives. De facto military prerogatives were thus lower in mid-1987 in Uruguay than in Argentina.

Although Uruguay has "restored" an old model of civilian control, we should bear in mind that the parameters of the Uruguayan polity are in fact different from those in the early 1960s. The Left is larger and now more institutionally embedded in the party system. The questions about structural changes in the economy, questions that were placed on the agenda in the mid-1960s, remain on the agenda. Also, notwithstanding Uruguay's return to a previous model of civilian control, the hard reality is that the military is now politically aware of its potential power and watches politics carefully from the sidelines. As an institution, the Uruguayan military in the late 1980s is different from the early 1960s in two key respects. They are now more organizationally and doctrinally structured around intelligence and internal-security missions. The old civil-military model in fact never addressed these two issues. Furthermore, in the judgment of President Sanguinetti and his key advisers, these issues are not central to the establishment of civilian control. The congruence between the model of civil-military control and the institutions to be controlled is thus not as tight as it was in the early 1960s.

## MILITARY PREROGATIVES IN SPAIN

For our purposes, one of the major things to be aware of about military prerogatives in Spain is that their peak was during the civil war when they were close to the maximum. But, as measured by a whole series of indicators, the influence of the military as an institution within the authoritarian regime had significantly eroded before Franco died. Military expenditures, which had been over half of the central budget immediately after World War II, oscillated around 22 to 28 percent from 1962 to 1975. Military ministers composed 50 percent of the first Cabinet after World War II. Between 1957 and 1962, they averaged around 43 percent of the Cabinet, but from 1969 to 1974 their figure was halved. Finally, in the last three Franco cabinets, the only ministers whose primary career identification had been the military were the three service ministers.[30]

In the judgment of Juan Linz and Fernando Rodrigo, for the last quarter-century of Franco's rule the military in Spain had effectively been removed from the direct exercise of political power.[31] Franco for most of his rule held three different positions concurrently: chief of state, head of the party, and *generalísimo* of the armed forces. He signed appointments under all three titles but predominately as chief of state. It is important to stress that the Spanish military had no recent exercise of political power similar to that exercised by the military as an institution in Brazil, Argentina, or Uruguay. The question of succession had also been to a great extent resolved by Franco before he died. In 1969 he had the Cortes declare Juan Carlos king. In 1973 Franco retained his position as head of state but created the office of "president of the government." Franco made arrangements so that after his death Juan Carlos would be head of state and commander in chief of the armed forces, and possess the right to appoint and promote officers.[32]

The Spanish transition thus began with fewer military prerogatives than in Brazil. Just as importantly, in Spain from 1975 to 1987 the government cautiously but steadily expanded its prerogatives in the area of military affairs. In July 1977 the three separate

[30] For tables on military budgets and Cabinet representation between 1940 and 1975, see the previously cited article by Bañón and Olmeda, "Las Fuerzas Armadas en España," 306–317.

[31] See two excellent articles by Fernando Rodrigo, "El Papel de las Fuerzas Armadas Españolas Durante la Transición Política: Algunas Hipótesis Básicas," and "Las Fuerzas Armadas y la Transición." The judgment of Juan Linz was made in a private commentary on an earlier draft of this work.

[32] See Rodrigo, "El Papel de las Fuerzas Armadas Españolas . . . ," 350–356, for the elaborate and well thought-out effort by Franco to invest Juan Carlos with authority vis-à-vis the military.

service Ministries were replaced by a unified Ministry of Defense whose first incumbent was the former Chief of the Army Staff, General Gutiérrez Mellado. Fortunately, General Gutiérrez Mellado had the wide respect both of the Prime Minister, Adolfo Suárez, and of the army. Gutiérrez Mellado's tenure built compliance for the new institution. In 1981, when the first civilian Minister of Defense assumed office, it was not seen as a drastic blow to military prerogatives. Another important change concerned the Code of Military Justice. Revisions to the code were discussed extensively by the Cortes and were eventually written into law in October 1980. The law sharply reduced the jurisdiction of military courts and established the right of appeal to the highest civilian court. There has also been a gradual but very significant distancing of the military from internal-security and police functions. The Minister of the Interior tightly controls the orders for dispatching armed police. In April 1978 a civilian was made director of security. Finally, for the first time since the Guardia Civil was created in the mid-nineteenth century, in spring 1986 a civilian was made its director-general.

The process of gradual civilian empowerment for over a decade has allowed the government to address in routine ways situations that might have otherwise deteriorated. Civilian-directed police are the major forces fighting against Basque guerrillas, and the authority of the civilian Minister of the Interior seems unchallenged by the military. Nowhere was the dialectic of civilian power creation and the narrowing of military prerogatives clearer than in the case of the trials that followed the February 1981 coup attempt. The government was massively backed after the coup attempt by demonstrations in the street. Public-opinion polls clearly showed that the military claim to represent a silent majority was false. Only 2 percent of the Spaniards who were polled said they were in favor of military government.[33] The previously estab-

---

[33] For a discussion of this and other public opinion polls, see the previously cited manuscript by Linz and Stepan, "The Political Crafting of Democratic Consolidation and Destruction."

lished right of appeal to the highest civilian courts enabled the government to appeal rapidly the light sentences the convicted military rebels received. In the judgment of Juan Linz, the 1983 appeal trial and the attendant publicity were highly beneficial for the consolidation of democracy. New costs for military attempts to usurp power had been established, and civilian prerogatives to control the military democratically were asserted and accepted.[34]

CONCLUSION

When we combine both the dimension of articulated conflict and the dimension of military prerogatives and attempt to make a rough approximation of the location of our four countries, we get the configuration in Figure 7.3. What is clear from this figure is that Spain is the only country that is close to establishing a mutually accepted model of democratic control of the military. In Latin America, Uruguay has made substantial progress in redemocratizing military prerogatives, but the intensity and effectiveness of military resistance to their physical appearance in courts on human-rights charges raised Uruguay on the contestation dimension and requires a location on the prerogative dimension not much better than midway on the chart. In Argentina, the military's formal prerogatives have been reduced but, as the military has begun to reconstitute itself after its post-Malvinas disarray, articulated military contestation has increased. *De jure*, Argentina appears to have reduced prerogatives as much as Uruguay, but *de facto* the civilian government is less able than is Uruguay to exercise its prerogatives. Brazil, which looked roughly similar to Spain on the contestation dimension, is the country that is most different from Spain on the prerogative dimension and, of the four

---

[34] For civil-military relations during the Spanish transition, see the previously cited works by Boyd and Boyden, "The Armed Forces and the Transition to Democracy in Spain," and Payne, "Modernization of the Armed Forces." I am also indebted to Rafael Bañón for sending me the manuscript of his forthcoming article, "Las Fuerzas Armadas en la Transición Política Española: 1975–1985."

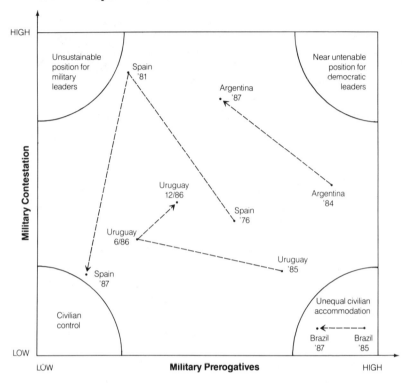

Figure 7.3 Post-transition evolution in Brazil, Argentina, Uruguay, and Spain.

High conflict points in Argentina were the 1987 Easter-week mutinies.

High conflict point in Spain was the February 1981 coup attempt.

High conflict point in Uruguay was the crisis precipitated by the military's assertion that they would not appear before civilian courts to face human-rights violations charges in December 1986.

countries we have studied, has the greatest amount of military prerogatives.

From a theoretical and comparative perspective, what are some of the implications for Brazil of the fact that it remained in an "unequal civilian accommodation" position for the first two years of civilian rule?

The first thing we must ask is whether Brazil should be called a democracy. There are many countries, such as contemporary Honduras and Guatemala, that combine high military prerogatives and low articulated conflict but which, in my judgment, fall outside the box of democratic politics because military power in the polity is so clearly dominant. The fact that Brazil is on the margin of not being a democracy is reinforced by the fact that to my knowledge there is at present no other democracy in the world that warrants location with Brazil in the "unequal civilian accommodation" category.[35]

The structural vulnerability of Brazil's position is compounded when we consider other normative and contextual issues. For many people democratization should entail formal procedural guarantees and the deepening of the substantive content of democracy. With the latter point in mind, it is useful to recognize that of the democracies in the world, the two democracies with the largest number of citizens who live in absolute poverty are India and Brazil. However, Brazil has a much worse distribution of income than India. In the early 1980s, the bottom 40 percent of the population in India received 16.2 percent of the nation's wealth; in Brazil

---

[35] In the late 1970s both Portugal and Nigeria were probably in this category. The Portuguese constitution, issued two years after the April 1974 revolution, gave extraordinary prerogatives to the predominantly military Council of the Revolution. Article 148 stated that the Council of the Revolution would be competent to "Make laws and regulations concerning the organization, functioning, and discipline of the armed forces. . . ." It also stated that "the powers referred to in . . . the foregoing paragraph shall be vested in the Council of the Revolution alone." Article 149, paragraph 3, asserted flatly: "Decree-laws of the Council of the Revolution shall have the same validity as laws of the Assembly of the Republic or the decree-laws of the government, and its implementing decrees have the same validity as implementing decrees of the government." Nigeria was also probably in this category of "unequal accommodation." Nigeria moved out of this category as a result of a coup. Portugal moved out of this category in 1982 when the two largest parties acted in concert to introduce a constitutional change that abolished the Council of the Revolution. At the same time, they passed a new defense law that elaborated a variety of institutional procedures for greater civilian control of the military. Senior-officer willingness to accept these new legal arrangements may have been increased because of their desire to reduce the power of junior officers and thus strengthen the chain of command.

they received only 7 percent.[36] In fact, Brazil may well have the worst distribution of income of any democracy in the world.[37]

When I discussed the vulnerabilities of "unequal civilian accommodation" in formal terms, I mentioned that, given a high degree of military prerogatives, there was the possibility that socioeconomic or political conflict in the polity could lead toward a nondemocratic resolution by a variety of paths, such as a "white coup," a civilian-led "garrison state," or a dangerous loss of legitimacy. In Brazil during a very politically and economically difficult period in May–June 1987, elements of all three of these vulnerabilities became manifest and were widely and publicly discussed.[38]

Another logical vulnerability of an unequal civilian accommo-

[36] Figures cited in Edmar Bacha and Herbert S. Klein, eds., *A Transição Incompleta: Brasil Desde 1945*, 20.

[37] To put Brazil's income distribution in global perspective, in a World Bank study of ten middle-income countries of the world, democratic and nondemocratic, Brazil had substantially the worst income distribution. In 1972 the bottom two deciles of Brazil's population had 2 percent of the nation's wealth. Only Mexico, with 2.9 percent, was remotely close to Brazil. In the Philippines the bottom two deciles of the population had 5.2 percent of the nation's wealth, in South Korea they had 5.7 percent, and in Indonesia 6.6 percent. See World Bank, *World Development Report* (1984). For a detailed analysis of income distribution in Brazil, see Helga Hoffmann, "Pobreza e Propriedade no Brazil: O que Está Mundando?"

[38] In the aftermath of the collapse of Brazil's stabilization plan and with inflation in May 1987 approaching an annualized rate of 1,000 percent a year, more than 60 percent of the electorate polled in Rio and São Paulo wanted direct elections to be held in 1988, which would have reduced President Sarnay's mandate by two years. See "Rio e São Paulo só Dão 4 Anos para Sarney," *Jornal do Brasil*, May 25, 1987. The timing of direct presidential elections was being widely discussed in the constituent assembly, and significant leaders of civil and political society assumed that the constituent assembly would be sovereign on this issue or, at the very least, would play a powerful and legitimate role in binding and consensual negotiations. However, President Sarney, after extensive private discussions with military leaders and with virtually no consultation with Congress or with civilian political leaders, went on television and unilaterally announced that he had decided that he would yield one year of his inherited mandate but that direct presidential elections would not be held until November 1989. For the next few weeks, many of Brazil's major publications showed cartoons with President Sarney either dressed in military attire or totally surrounded by uniformed officers.

dation position is that the democratic electoral process can produce an electoral mandate for major change that includes a significant reduction of military prerogatives. This presents the
possibility that the civil-military model would very probably move
into the upper right-hand corner (high prerogatives, high conflict)
of Figure 7.3. This is a difficult civil-military position to sustain,
and a nondemocratic resolution of the conflict is a significant
threat.

With these observations in mind, it is useful to remember that
in a very important respect Brazil has still undergone only an in-
complete transition. The chief executive has not yet been produced by a direct election. In the not-too-distant future, if Brazil
is to remain even a formal democracy it will have to have a direct
presidential election that will have the following characteristics: it
will be the first direct presidential election since 1960; it will be
the first presidential election in which illiterates will vote; it will
be the first election since the television era (more households in
Rio have television than running water).[39] It will be held in a political system with historically weak party identification. To be
sure, in most of the recent redemocratization elections in southern
Europe and Latin America (and in gubernatorial and legislative
elections in Brazil), moderates have won. However, significant
civilian and military elites in Brazil harbor worries about the upcoming presidential election. Thus both groups of elites contain
some members who are reluctant to see military prerogatives di-
minished.

Brazilian civil-military relations have a further complicating
factor. Some of Brazil's historic reform movements (abolition of
the Empire, the 1930 revolution, the nationalization of petroleum,
the import-substitution drive) were aided by strong military leadership. In the recent struggle for the retention of a "market reserve" for Brazil's domestic computer industry, the left and the
military were again allies. The Brazilian military thus has signifi-

[39] See Fernando Henrique Cardoso, "Associated-Dependent Development and
Democratic Theory."

cant ideological and alliance capabilities that help them in their effort to retain prerogatives.

Unlike Uruguay or Spain, in Brazil one of the greatest sources of structural instability resides in the civil-military model itself. For a variety of reasons, there are significant civilian and military actors who accept high military prerogatives. Nevertheless, given the existence of high military prerogatives, and the fact that these prerogatives could be electorally or socially challenged, the potential for civil-military conflict remains high. This reality feeds back into the system as a series of informal pressures as to who should, or should not, be nominated for president. This feedback system, not unrelated to the existence of high military prerogatives, is present in Brazil to a degree simply not found in Spain, Argentina, or Uruguay.

The analysis of military prerogatives and their impact on politics probably deserve more attention than they have received. Though we have no studies on the subject of comparative prerogatives, such studies might shed light over some key issues concerning civilian control. For example, most analysts are surprised by the relatively successful advances toward civilian control in the Dominican Republic since the death of Trujillo. The Dominican Republic upon Trujillo's death seemed to have almost nothing in its favor concerning potential for democratization. But since the civil war of 1965 there has been no military government. Furthermore, since President Guzmán was elected in 1978, the Dominican Republic has been a democracy. More surprising, in a recent study of military autonomy in twenty Latin American countries, only two were classified as having "effective subordination according to a liberal democratic model"—Venezuela and the Dominican Republic.[40] My hypothesis is that part of the explanation for this surprising result is the fact that the military as an institution has never in the history of the Dominican Republic had significant autonomous prerogatives. Under Trujillo the military virtually had

[40] Juan Rial, "Las Fuerzas Armadas en tanto Actor Político en los Procesos de (Re) Construcción de la Democracia en América Latina," appendix.

no prerogatives or professional autonomy at all.[41] Mexico is not democratic, but one of the explanations for the strong civilian control is that at no time in its history did the military rule the country as an institution with the high degree of professional prerogatives routinely found in many other Latin American countries.

The other side of this theoretical coin is that in those countries that have had extensive experience of high control of the polity by the military, the question of civilian control, especially democratic civilian control, emerges as an especially salient issue.

I asked a former Brazilian General Staff colonel why he thought the civilians had made no progress toward controlling the military since the transition. He said, "The military have a project and the will. The civilians have neither."[42] In terms of our initial discussion, it is clear that the military have reconstituted themselves to maneuver as a political actor under democracy. In Brazil, in the area of democratic management of force, I believe it is fair to say that democratic groups in civil society, in political society, and in the state are only now beginning the effort to constitute themselves as actors.

In democratic theory, politics is about free contestation via elections for the control of state power. However, if the military has great prerogatives over the management of violence, an intrinsic dimension of the modern state is outside the control and scope of democratic politics.

In all polities that would be democracies, actors in civil society, political society, and the state must pay specific attention to strategies of empowerment so that they can enhance their capacity to manage force democratically. This is the subject of my concluding chapter.

[41] For telling details of the complete lack of autonomy of the military under Trujillo, see Robert D. Crassweller, *Trujillo: The Life and Times of a Caribbean Dictator.* For example, Trujillo went from being a newly commissioned second lieutenant with no formal training in 1919 to Chief of Staff in 1924 (pp. 48–49). When his son Ramfis was four years old he was made a full colonel, at nine he was made a brigadier general, (p. 130). For the military after Trujillo, see G. Pope Atkins, *Arms and Politics in the Dominican Republic.*

[42] Interview, not for direct attribution.

CHAPTER **8**

# Democratic Empowerment and the Military: The Tasks of Civil Society, Political Society, and the State

THIS TOPIC needs extensive treatment, serious thought, and frank discussion by all theorists and practitioners concerned with the consolidation of democracy. What follows are some preliminary thoughts on what should be a major debate.

## CIVIL SOCIETY

Democracy is about the open contestation for power via elections, and the oversight and control of state power by the representatives of the people. In virtually all polities of the world, and very much so in Latin America, the military are a permanent factor in any calculus of power. Therefore, in a democracy, civil society must consider how it can make a contribution to the democratic control of military and intelligence systems. It is an obvious point but one that bears repeating: the capacity of the military as a complex institution to develop a consensus for intervention is greatly aided to the extent that civil society "knocks on the doors" of the barracks. In 1964 in Brazil, and in Chile in 1973, many powerful representatives of civil society—including the church—"knocked on the door" and created the "Brumairean moment." The transitional military governments hoped for by many middle-class and upper-class members of civil society became long-lasting bureaucratic-authoritarian regimes with significant interests of their own. It is important to understand, theoretically and politically, that this phenomenon is one of the predictable consequences of "knocking on the door," and that "Brumairean moments" can turn into praetorian decades. This fundamental point aside, what else is important for civil society to consider? Obviously, it is extremely important that civil society revalorize democracy as a permanent value and not just as a temporary tactic.[1] The forging of political institutions that have increased strength, autonomy, and legitimacy is also clearly critical. Books can and should be written on all of these problems.

Turning specifically to the technical capacities of civil society vis-à-vis the military and intelligence systems, what could be done that has not really been done in the past? Let us return to our discussion of the "liberal bias." Latin American social scientists have become the leaders of the world social-science community in conceptualizing the realities and implications of the new global political economy. They have also done some of the best work in the world on social movements and popular culture. However, until recently, the formal study of military organizations and international relations—especially geopolitics, and most specifically the study of territorial disputes and military strategy—has been neglected. Those civilians who have concerned themselves with these matters have tended to be professors who attended institutions such as the Escola Superior de Guerra in Brazil or Argentina's Escuela de Defensa Nacional, where the intellectual agenda was set by the military and where, sanctioned by national security doctrine, French, U.S., and Latin American military Cold War and internal subversion preoccupations were dominant. This situation has often meant that few members of the democratic opposition in civil society were specialists on military matters or wrote alternative geopolitical works. In Argentina, especially, this served to privilege the military's perception of the country's geomilitary problems.

Most major democracies have at least one major civilian-led independent research institute that concentrates on international military politics. In the United States the Brookings Institution has often supplied authoritative and well-researched expert, alternative assessments of military strategy. In India and in England, the Institute for Defense Studies and Analysis and the International

[1] On the important subject of the revalorization by much of the Brazilian Left of democratic procedures, see Francisco Weffort, "Why Democracy?"

Institute for Strategic Studies, respectively, perform a comparable function. The creation of such prestigious, independent, and civilian-led institutes—and comparable journals—would seem to be high on the agenda of civil society.

Latin American universities, to date, have failed to incorporate military sociology and military strategy routinely into their curricula. This is a vital task because the newspapers, television, and weekly press should have military experts on their staffs. Equally important, the constant academic production of a cadre of citizens who are masters in their knowledge of the force structure, organizational style, budgetary issues, doctrinal questions, and the specific details of weapons systems are indispensable for the fulfillment of the military and intelligence oversight functions of political society, especially in the legislative branch.

To illustrate the vital importance of developing capacities in civil society to participate in debates about the role of the military, in order to help create an environment conducive to democratic civilian control, let us return to our analysis of constitution making. In Brazil, the subcommission of the Constituent Assembly that wrote the draft legislation (*anteprojeto*) on the role of the military held eight hearings that lasted a total of forty-two hours.[2] In most of the other subcommissions of the Constituent Assembly, a wide variety of groups from civil society lobbied hard to be heard and forcefully presented their suggestions. Astoundingly, however, of the total of twenty-three individuals who managed to present testimony before the subcommittee concerned with the constitutional role of the military, only two represented independent, and in any way critical, groups from civil society. One person was the president of the Brazilian Bar Association. The other was a representative from Brazil's first major academic research program devoted to military issues.[3] Of the twenty-one other people

---

[2] Subcomissão de Defesa do Estado, da Sociedade e de Sua Segurança, *Anteprojeto: Relatório*, p.3.

[3] The academic representive was himself a recently retired colonel, Geraldo Cavagnari. He is rapidly emerging as one of Brazil's most incisive and critical commentators on civil-military affairs. He represented the Núcleo de Estudos Estratégicos, Universidade Estadual de Campinas.

who presented testimony, all but one (a retired general) currently worked for military, police, or intelligence organizations. Four came from the Escola Superior de Guerra, four from the General Staff of the armed forces, two from the National Security Council, three from the Federal Police, five from the state military police, one from the military police association, and the one speaker simply labeled as a ''Personality'' was an active-duty general.[4] In addition to these presentations, the military conducted an extensive publications campaign. Near the end of the military regime the army had created a Center for Social Communications to work directly for the Minister of the Army. This center generated and circulated widely a twenty-nine page pamphlet, *Temas Constitucionais* (Constitutional Themes), which forcefully presented the army case on all major constitutional issues concerning civil-military relations.[5]

The central point that emerges from analysis of the pamphlet, and from our previous discussion of military discourse and prerogatives, is that the Brazilian military entered the New Republic with a sense of their legitimate role (with a ''role-belief'') that entails deep, permanent involvement in managing conflict in the polity.[6]

[4] *Anteprojeto: Relatório*, 3.

[5] Centro de Comunicação Social do Exército, *Temas Constitucionais*.

[6] J. Samuel Fitch, in a recent paper, identified five ''ideal-types'' of military role-beliefs. He argued, correctly, that ''Role-beliefs specify the condition under which political action by the military is 'legitimate' and define the range of permissible military actions in a crisis situation. Given the inevitability of such crises, institutionalization of a democratic regime requires institutionalization of less interventionist role-beliefs.'' From the least to most interventionist, the ideal-types were (1) classic professionalism, (2) democratic professionalism, (3) constitutional guardians, (4) guardians of national interest, (5) guardians of national security. Since the late nineteenth century at the least, the Brazilian military's self-image has always been more interventionist than is called for under ''democratic professionalism.'' After 1889, as we have seen, Brazilian constitutions have always given the military a role in maintaining internal order. Brazil's ''moderating pattern'' of civil-military relations between 1945 and 1964 fell between the ideal types of ''constitutional guardians'' and ''guardians of national interest.'' With the development of the doctrines and institutions associated with ''the new professionalism of internal security and national development,'' which we analyzed in Chapter 2 and which were added to the ''moderating pattern'' legacy, the Brazilian

Military leaders and theoreticians have worked extremely hard, within the military schooling system and within critical sectors of the polity, to gain ideological acceptance for their various self-defined roles. Therefore, if an alternative, less interventionist "democratic professional" model of civil-military relations is to gain acceptance within civil society, and eventually by the military because it is the law of the land and conducive to such professional military goals as hierarchy, depoliticization, and distance from police missions, it will require intense technical, conceptual, and ideological work by many groups in civil society.[7]

There has not yet been such intense work in Brazilian civil society. In the absence of such a politically powerful and technically competent counterdiscourse, the military discourse about national security, as analyzed in Chapter 5 and as was substantially reproduced in the army's *Temas Constitucionais*, was not displaced in the anteprojeto for the new constitution. On the contrary, the dominant discourse in the chairman's preamble was surprisingly close to standard Escola Superior de Guerra national security doctrine and terminology. "Opposition" was accepted, but "contestation" was not. The standard ESG critique of the excesses of "liberal states" was repeated, as was the ESG argument that "contes-

military developed a self-image that falls between the "guardians of national interest" and "guardians of national security." Fitch's ideal-types and important discussion are found in his "Theoretical Model: Core Assumptions; Assessment of Civil-Military Tensions and Short-term Coup Risk." Working draft prepared for the Inter-American Dialogue, Washington, D.C. (May 1987).

[7] In any particular polity, whatever variant of a "democratic-professional" model is strived for, some provision for the routine and legitimate incorporation of military advice on matters of national defense is called for. In Fitch's ideal-typical version, he defines "democratic-professionalism" as follows: "In this view, military officers are viewed as professionals within the military component of national defense, which is recognized as having other components as well. Political involvements are not only unprofessional but contrary to the military officer's individual and collective obligation to defend the democratic state, to which he owes his highest loyalty. As a citizen and a soldier, the officer accepts his subordination to the constitutionally defined authorities and accepts the right and duty of those authorities to define military and defense policy. Military officers are viewed as policy advisors in matters within their realm of expertise and as implementors of the policies adopted through constitutionally proscribed procedures."

tation'' was inherently a greater problem for democracies in developing countries than in developed, democratic countries. The ESG "principle of self-defense" was reaffirmed, as was the necessity for "safeguards" and a continued role for the military in internal defense.[8]

This book will go to press before the final version of the Brazilian constitution is accepted. However, even if the new constitution reverses some of the recommendations of the military's constitutional proposal, it is clear that the struggle to create hegemony in civil society for a democratic model of civil-military relations has only begun.

## POLITICAL SOCIETY

Most major stable democracies have crafted, over time, permanent standing committees in their legislatures, or in their party-based parliamentary cabinets, which are devoted exclusively to the routine oversight and monitoring of their countries' military and intelligence systems. These committees characteristically have professional staffs specializing in matters of military strategy, budgeting, and intelligence. Often these staffs are drawn from the ranks of both the professional civil service and from the political parties.

The party-based parliamentary cabinet tradition is almost non-existent in Latin America. Therefore, if the oversight and monitoring tasks in Latin America are to be carried out by political society, the most likely forum is the legislative branch. However, in Latin American legislatures, permanent committees with large staffs and independent research capacities often either do not exist or are understaffed and have few resources. What is needed, therefore, is a deliberate strategy for the *empowerment* of legislatures so that they are in a position to carry out their military and intelligence oversight functions in a routine, democratic fashion.

Military, intelligence, or defense ministry officials do occasionally appear before legislatures in Latin America. But usually this

---

[8] See *Anteprojeto: Relatório*, 22–31.

occurs under the circumstances of a *special commission of inquiry* established to examine a particular controversy. From the perspective of comparative civil-military relations in a democracy, this is a dangerous and ineffective review mechanism for two reasons. First, precisely because it is ad hoc and not a standing committee, legislative leaders are not supported by a cadre of professional staff members with expert knowledge of the intricacies of the field. Second, by its very nature, an ad hoc special commission of inquiry occurs in a controversial, conflictual setting that tends to increase the latent paranoia most military organizations throughout the world have about political "interference" in their professional activities. Thus a primary requirement must be to reduce the atmosphere of *exceptional* confrontational inquiry, by making the defense ministers or the military's appearance before legislative leaders a routine occurrence. If political party leaders know that these permanent standing committees are a routine yet important part of legislative life, some members of all parties will attempt to acquire special expertise in these areas so as to be able to conduct or chair these committee meetings in a respectful, but deeply authoritative, manner. The routinization of legislative-military transactions can help reduce mutual fears and ignorance of military and party leaders alike. In short, the *self-empowerment of legislatures* in national security matters is both politically necessary and politically possible.

In Brazil, under the new civilian regime, the military have made an intensive effort to empower themselves to advocate their policies before the legislative branch. The military has assigned thirteen officers, all General Staff school graduates, to work full time, to act as liaison officers and advisors on military matters, and to lobby the Congress.[9] All thirteen officers have permanent offices in the Congress. They attend virtually all hearings relevant to mil-

[9] Interviews with army and navy officers in their official "Parliamentary Advisor" offices, Brasília, June 2, 1987. The army has assigned five General Staff school graduates, the navy and the air force each have assigned three, and the General Staff of the armed forces maintains two. These thirteen officers in turn have support staffs in their congressional offices and receive some assistance from their home ministries.

itary affairs and to national security, as they broadly conceive the subjects. They also coordinate an extensive program that provides at times lavish trips for congressmen to see military or development projects, such as offshore oil sites that the military deem relevant to national security.[10] The military have constructed what is possibly the largest and best organized "lobby" in the Brazilian Congress.

On the other hand, the Brazilian Congress has not yet taken any steps to empower itself to be an informed and authoritative actor concerning military affairs. Both chambers of the Congress have a "Committee on National Security," but congressional committees, as such, are not assigned a permanent staff. The Senate has a permanent Central Staff of approximately ninety professional advisors. However, in the judgment of one professional advisor, who has also done research on comparative legislative practices, none of the ninety advisors have been recruited because of their interest or technical capacity in military affairs. Indeed, his summary judgment was that "for the last two years no staffer has spent two minutes thinking about how Congress can organize itself to monitor, supervise or control the military or the intelligence services."[11]

A retired army colonel who as recently as 1985 was Sub-Chief for Strategy of the army General Staff, and who now is a critic of the dangers of military autonomy, argues that the Congress has no effective control over such issues as military budgets, which, by law, it can in theory review. "What is lacking is technical competence for the Congress to debate military affairs and projects. . . . Why? Because these matters are not widely debated by society."[12]

Political society could do more to empower itself to help create

---

[10] Various members of the Constituent Assembly commented on these trips in my interviews in Brasilia, May 31 to June 4, 1987.

[11] Interview with Eduardo Jorge Caldos Pereira, Brasília, June 1, 1987. When I interviewed him, he was on assignment as advisor to the leader of the Government Party in the Senate.

[12] See the informative feature interview with Geraldo Cavagnari, in *Senhor*, May 19, 1987, 5–11.

a model of democratic-professionalism that would strive to reduce military autonomy and prerogatives. Such a model needs a base in the values, geopolitical perspectives, and technical capacities concerning military affairs of civil society.

This argument is reinforced when we consider the case of Argentina. Unlike the situation in Brazil, in Argentina there has been a major effort by the chief executive to forge a model of democratic control of the military. However, political society, especially Congress, has not played a powerful supporting role in helping to establish this model and make it routine. When Congress began to function in 1984, two or three full-time staff members were assigned to congressional committees dealing with military affairs. It was readily admitted, however, that none of these staff members were in any sense professionally prepared to analyze the military. Indeed, the Congress itself generated virtually no legislative requests for information from the military. One key congressman insisted that he had a budget to hire up to ten specialists to help on military affairs, but they simply were not to be found. In addition, very few congressmen who were members of the committees relating to the military visited any military installations or took an active interest in professional military issues.[13] The relative lack of informed policy concern and knowledge in the polity means that the continuous and robust support needed by President Alfonsín for his effort to make a new model of democratic civil-military control routine in Argentina is not yet in place. Fortunately, there are now unprecedented efforts by some members of civil and political society to begin to empower themselves to be actors in military affairs.

## THE STATE

To the extent that the military have a near technical monopoly concerning military expertise, the capacity of a democratic gov-

---

[13] The above is based on a number of interviews conducted with senators and deputies and congressional professional-staff members between 1984 and 1987 in Buenos Aires and in New York.

ernment to exercise a monopoly over the management of force within the state apparatus is extremely limited. Thus everything we have said about extending the range of people and institutions in civil and political society with a deep knowledge and concern about national defense and military affairs would help enrich the ideological, technical, and organizational resources democratic governments can call upon when they come into office.

Even if we assume that civil and political society begin the multiple tasks of empowerment, there are some tasks that the executive branch of the democratic state must attempt to carry out concerning the restructuring of the management of force within the state apparatus itself.[14] Let me formulate this restructuring problem by a hypothetical, but by no means unrealistic, case.

If the military retains control over numerous parts of the state apparatus such that it is inherently involved in the domestic management of political conflict (call this possibility "A"), and if the military has a working definition of democracy (especially regarding the legitimate role of conflict and the role of the military in the state management of these conflicts) that is different from the working definition held by democratically elected officials "in charge" of the state (call this possibility "B"), then serious intrastate conflict between the democratic government and the military is inevitable. One solution is for the government to abdicate state authority over these areas to the military. If this is done, the government is a "limited democracy" at best, and its legitimacy is eroded in those sectors of civil and political society that are thereby prevented from using the normal play of democratic conflict to advance their interests. Thus one of the greatest sources of strength of a new democracy—its legitimacy—is weakened. In such a situation of limited democracy and weakened legitimacy, change-oriented conflict outside the democratic system could increase, and civilian advocates of "stability" or the status quo may

---

[14] While still on active duty, and three months before the military left office, Colonel Geraldo Lesbat Cavagnari Filho wrote a controversial conference paper devoted to military autonomy within the state and strategies for the incoming civilian government to reduce such autonomy. "Abordagem Preliminar de uma Política para redução da Autonomia Militar no Estado," Brasília, January 3, 1985.

well appeal to the military to exercise their internal-security prerogatives or even possibly to assume power. It would be easier, in short, for civilian and military advocates of a coup to compose a winning coup coalition, thus allowing direct military intervention to begin again.

However, military involvement in the management of conflict also presents threats to military hierarchy because of the tendency of those military components most involved in repression and intelligence activity to become autonomous, and for military attention to professional tasks to be neglected. It is conceivable that the combination of legitimacy problems, growing opposition, threats to internal hierarchy, and the desire of the military as institution to devote attention to professional concerns and to avoid the risks of continued military government would contribute to military acquiesence in what they would see as the safest alternative ruling formula available to them—a new democratic regime, which would leave the military with substantial prerogatives within the state concerning the management of force. And thus the cycle would begin again.

For our purposes, the two critical elements are the initial military control over parts of the state apparatus involved in the management of domestic political conflict (A), and the military's role-belief and their working definition of democracy (B). To prevent the return of the cycle described above, the democratic leadership of the state must implement a well conceived, *politically led* strategy toward the military (a "política militar").

I stress "politically led" because in most democracies the chief executive of the state is the commander in chief of the military. Some of the chief executive's political powers as a persuader and a leader would have to be directed toward winning professional, not merely personal, allies within the military establishment. If the military as an institution is opposed to the model of "democratic professionalism," the chances of the cycle of military intervention and military extrication being repeated will be greatly increased. However, since repetition of the cycle also entails risks for the military as an institution, military awareness of such a threat could give the executive some potential to win adherents for an alternative policy.

A passive executive who abdicates responsibility would probably mean that any initial effort in the newly democratic regime to "reprofessionalize" the military would be militarily led. A purely negative executive, who devotes all his efforts to eliminating military prerogatives but neglects to play a leadership role in attempting to formulate and implement an alternative model of civil-military relations, would probably be locked in dangerous conflicts with the military. An executive who is positively involved in forging a role for the military that narrows their involvement in state regulation of conflict, builds effective procedures for civilian control, seeks to increase military professional capacities, and lessens the risks—for the polity and for the military—of further military intervention is what the theory and practice of democratization, would seem to indicate.[15]

Let us illustrate this argument by analyzing the Brazilian case. In Brazil the military have retained control over the peak intelligence service, the SNI, and the secretary-generalship of the National Security Council. These are two of the most powerful ad-

[15] In these terms, President Sarney in 1987 comes close to approximating a "passive executive." Although we lack a detailed documented analysis, my interviews in Venezuela in 1964 seemed to indicate that President Betancourt approximated an executive who was "positively involved" in all phases of constructing a more professionally competent military that would accept democratic civilian control. After the Easter-week mutinies of 1987 in Argentina, there was a growing concensus among President Alfonsín's closest advisors that the first part of his presidency had been characterized by "negative" executive action. However, they observed that to make a model of civilian control take hold, President Alfonsín would have to devote his great political energies to being "positively involved" in the attempt to build a more technically competent military and to work to make the military believe that he envisaged a permanent legitimate role for them within the Argentine state. A number of these advisors, in private interviews, commented that President Alfonsín had been crucial in winning acceptance for the "Plan Austral" in the economic sphere, and that the second half of his presidency should be devoted to forging and leading a "política militar" in the military sphere. Some of these advisors noted that President Alfonsín (and they) had not yet developed an overall "política militar," and that the absence of such a policy was aggravating civil-military relations.

ministrative clusters attached to the office of the presidency. The fact that the civilian president again and again utilizes these military-controlled institutions contributes to the "militarization" of the office of the presidency. It also helps to legitimate the routine involvement of the military in state management of internal conflict. In terms of our analysis, nothing has been done to reduce the initial military control over those parts of the state apparatus that manage domestic conflict (A). The executive has also done nothing to alter the military doctrine of security or to modify military role-beliefs, the second critical element I have identified (B).

If a president were to be directly elected in Brazil, and if he wanted to have a strategy to alter both A and B, what in theory could he do at the level of the state? Knowing that there will be military resistance, what sources of military support could the president draw upon in restructuring the relations of power?

The first area to examine would be the system of intelligence. Every major democracy in the world has intelligence services. In Chapter 2, I indicated how—without attacking, dismantling, or, for the most part, demoralizing their intelligence systems—England, France, and the United States have crafted mechanisms for the democratic management, monitoring, and oversight of their intelligence systems. In Brazil, even using the existing laws drafted by the military regime, the New Republic could eventually demilitarize the four top offices in the SNI—none of which are required by law to be occupied by military officers—which would remove the army from direct control of the intelligence system. This action would not be received well in the security community, but, if properly handled, many professional officers might welcome the initiative, because the belief that the SNI collects dossiers on individual officers and heavily influences promotion patterns, for reasons that may be extraneous to the officers' own professional capacity but of direct interest to the SNI's own bureaucratic concerns, is widespread.[16]

---

[16] Interestingly, in a wide-ranging discussion on this point, the military "parliamentary advisors" I interviewed did not put up a strong defense for the maintenance of the SNI under direct military control, or for the maintenance of the ministerial status of the chief of the SNI. They said these were political choices a

The second area for analysis is the National Security Council. Liberal political activists in much of Latin America dislike the very idea of a National Security Council. However, since the military are part of the state apparatus and national defense is a state function, some form of National Security Council, or its functional equivalent, is not inappropriate. Indeed, if the endeavor is to establish democratic civil-military relations, a National Security Council would seem politically useful for that endeavor for two reasons. First, in the absence of a forum for high-level discussions of national security, the traditional military argument that the only members of the polity who are deeply concerned with national defense and security are the military gains weight. Second, military involvement in a National Security Council would ensure that the military's function as advisor and potential implementor of policy is incorporated into the routine democratic institutions of the state.

The key point, of course, is that such a council be democratically controlled by *civilians*, and that the military participate as *advisors* to the civilian leadership. In the Brazilian army's pamphlet *Temas Constitucionais*, referred to earlier, the military recommended the retention of the National Security Council. Implicitly recognizing that many members of the Constituent Assembly considered the existing National Security Council a military-dominated vehicle, they made a suggestion that the presidents of the Chamber of Deputies, of the Senate, and of the Supreme Federal Court be added to the Council.[17] They were silent, however, on the central point: Who effectively controls the National Security Council? The current head of the National Security secretariat is also, as we have seen, both a general and the minister of the Military Household. This general supervises the many subdirectorates of the Council, the majority of whose heads are also active-duty officers, normally colonels. The permanent staff of the NSC is thus militarized and has significant agenda-shaping power. The offices

president had a right to make. The army pamphlet, *Temas Constitucionais*, although it robustly argues for and against numerous possible changes in civil-military relations, does not comment on the question of the SNI.

[17] *Temas Constitucionais*, 11.

of the secretary-general of the National Security Council and the head of the Military Household could be (as they have been at times in the past) held by two different people. The secretary-general could be made a non-Cabinet-rank civilian who could appoint professionally qualified civilian specialists to coordinate most of the subdirectorates, and the head of the Military Household could revert to the nonministerial status the position had before the military regime.

If the chief executive followed such a strategy, two of the major sources of military involvement in the state monitoring and regulating of conflict would be substantially reduced, and two of the six military cabinet ministers eliminated. A major step forward in demilitarizing the office of the presidency would also have been taken.

The post-Malvinas concern of Latin American militaries, especially in Brazil, to upgrade their professional capacity for joint operations may present a propitious argument for changes in the military's representation in democratic governments. Given the military's appreciation of the importance of effective, joint interservice professional operational capacity, and their recognition that historic interservice rivalry makes such joint operations virtually impossible, it is conceivable that eventually in Brazil a single Minister of Defense could replace the traditional Ministers of the Army, Navy, Air Force, and Joint General Staff. Politically, this would be easiest to implement if some net new resources for joint operations were added to the budget, and if the president—as commander in chief—and the new Minister of Defense were seen as actively engaged in a significant upgrading of the military capacity for joint operations.[18] If it were made clear that the new Minister of Defense would be a civilian, air force and navy anxiety about being dominated by an army minister would be reduced.

---

[18] In Argentina, where a Minister of Defense position has been created, the absence of significant new resources for joint operations and the military's perception that President Alfonsín is not actively engaged in supporting joint operations reforms have contributed to the military's passive noncompliance with many of the Ministry of Defense's initiatives.

If such a change in the state structure occurred, the remaining four military ministers would have been removed from the Cabinet. I do not mean to imply that these administrative arrangements by themselves would eliminate civil-military tension. However, given the fact that almost inevitably military leaders have a somewhat different attitude toward politics than elected officials, especially toward the role of allowable conflict in society, the removal of military ministers would diminish military ambivalence about policy coresponsibility. There are normally many policy measures the military might accept as a matter of hierarchy but could not bring themselves to advocate politically.

A final word should be said about doctrinal orientation. Where the military is a part of the state apparatus and has a markedly different idea about the nature of democratic politics and the legitimate role of the military than that held by the leaders of the government, this can be a major source of intrastate division. The executive team of the state apparatus will then, at some time, have to play an active role in monitoring and reshaping military resocialization. In post-World War II Germany, for example, the government created a major new military schooling system. In Uruguay, the president and the Minister of Defense temporarily closed ESEDENA, the war college most involved in formulating national security doctrine. In Argentina, President Alfonsín appointed a civilian head of the Escuela de Defesa Nacional. In Brazil, the government has taken no initiatives whatsoever concerning professional socialization patterns or doctrinal formulations relating to defense.

The war colleges in Brazil, Argentina, and Uruguay that developed national-security doctrines had a number of general characteristics. They were financed and directed by the military, normally the Joint General Staff. Civilians were admitted as students and professors, but the entire process was under direct military control. In the curriculum there was a great utilization of social-science terms in the war colleges, but the goal was not to use competing theories to inform analyses. Rather, the permanent staff were engaged in a constant effort to produce a sanctioned doctrine of state power. In this deformed social science, social and political conflicts were not accepted as a constituent element of a democracy. The recurrent assumption was that conflicts are dangerous. According to the national security doctrine, the state was viewed as an agent for structuring civil and political society so as to *dissuade* the articulation of conflict where possible, and to *repress* such articulation when necessary. In both dissuasion and repression, the military was seen as providing critical state resources, resources that could only be guaranteed if the military had a substantial degree of autonomy within the state. In these war colleges, technical matters of defense, such as force structure, weapons systems, military budgets, systems of command and control, and the logistics of joint operations received very little attention.

Ideologies that are dominant are seldom eliminated merely by negative actions, even state actions. The democratic leadership of the state will have to play a role in creating new doctrines of national defense that provide a positive alternative. In the post bureaucratic-authoritarian context of Brazil, Argentina, Uruguay, and eventually Chile, this may very well involve the creation of national-defense colleges under a civilian Minister of Defense. Such colleges might well include a curriculum with not less social science, but with more serious attention given by social scientists to the inevitable role of conflict in any polity. Such colleges also might feature much deeper professional concern with the technical dimensions of modern defense. The Ministry of Defense could select both the student body and the professorate, and both could contain civilian and military personnel. Graduates of these schools could provide professional cadres for the Ministry of Defense as well as for the general staffs of the armed forces. Obviously, the technical and professional capacity of the civilian Ministry of Defense to run such national-defense colleges will be greatly enhanced if civil society carries out the multiple tasks of self-empowerment in military matters that we have already discussed.

In summation, increasing effective control of the military and intelligence systems requires an effort by civil and political society to empower themselves to increase their own capacity for control. Within the state, a paradoxical mix of fewer military appointments that are inherently political in character, and more systematic professional incorporation of the military into civilian-led national-security councils and national-defense colleges, might reduce the military's sense of isolation and create a more effective system of mutual exchange of information and grievances, and thus enhance the capacity for democratic control.

# BIBLIOGRAPHY

Abramovay, Ricardo. "O Velho Poder dos Barões da Terra." In *Nova República: Um Balanço*, edited by Flavio Koutzii, pp. 204–226. São Paulo: L & PM Editores, 1986.

Abreu, Hugo. *O Outro Lado do Poder*. Rio de Janeiro: Editora Nova Fronteira, 1979.

Alvarez, Sonia E. "Politicizing Gender and Engendering Democracy." In *Democratizing Brazil: Problems of Transition and Consolidation*, edited by Alfred Stepan. New York: Oxford University Press, forthcoming.

Alves, Maria Helena Moreira. *Estado e Oposição no Brasil (1964–1984)*. Petrópolis: Editora Vozes, 1984.

Argentina. Comisión Nacional Sobre la Desaparación de Personas. *Nunca Más*. Buenos Aires: Editorial Universitaria de Buenos Aires, 1985.

Aristotle. *The Politics*, trans. by E. Barker. New York: Oxford University Press, 1962.

Arquidiocese de São Paulo. *Brasil: Nunca Mais*. Preface by D. Paulo Evaristo, Cardeal Arns. Petrópolis: Editora Vozes, 1985.

Arriagada H., Genaro. *El Pensamiento Político de los Militares (Estudios Sobre Chile, Argentina, Brasil y Uruguay)*. Santiago: Centro de Investigaciones Socioeconómicas, n.d.

———. *La Política Militar de Pinochet: 1973–1985*. Santiago: Salesianos, 1985.

Arruda, Antonio de. *ESG: História de Sua Doutrina*. Rio de Janeiro: Edições GRD em convênio com o Instituto Nacional do Livro e Ministério da Educação e Cultura, 1980.

Atkins, Pope G. *Arms and Politics in the Dominican Republic*. Boulder, Colorado: Westview Press, 1981.

Aubrey, Crispin. *Who's Watching You? Britain's Security Services and the Official Secrets Act*. Harmondsworth, Middlesex: Penguin, 1981.

Bacchus, Wilfred. "Long-Term Military Rulership in Brazil: Ideologic Consensus and Dissensus, 1963–1983." *Journal of Political and Military Sociology* 13 (Spring 1985): 99–123.

Bacha, Edmar L., and Klein, Herbert S., eds. *A Transição Incompleta: Brasil Desde 1945*. 2 vols. Rio de Janeiro and São Paulo: Editora Paz e Terra, 1986.

Bacha, Edmar L., and Malan, Pedro S. "Brazil's Debt: From the Miracle to the IMF." In *Democratizing Brazil: Problems of Transition and Consolidation*, edited by Alfred Stepan. New York: Oxford University Press, forthcoming.

Baker, Robert H. "Central Organizations of Defense in the Soviet Union." In *Central Organizations of Defense*, edited by Martin Edmonds. Boulder, Colorado: Westview Press, 1985.

Bañón, Rafael, and Olmeda, José Antonio. "Las Fuerzas Armadas en España: Institucionalización y Proceso de Cambio." In *La Institución Militar en el Estado Contemporáneo*, edited by Rafael Bañón and José Antonio Olmeda, pp. 270–325. Madrid: Editorial Alianza, 1985.

Barros, Alexandre de Souza Costa. "Brazil." In *Arms Production in Developing Countries: An Analysis of Decision Making*, edited by James Everett Katz, pp. 73–87. Lexington, Mass.: Lexington Books, 1984.

———. "The Brazilian Military: Professional Socialization, Political Performance, and State Building." Ph.D. dissertation, University of Chicago, 1978.

Barros, Alexandre de Souza Costa, and Coelho, Edmundo. "Military Intervention and Withdrawal in South America." *International Political Science Review* 2 (October 1981): 341–349.

Beltrám, Virgilio R. "Political Transition in Argentina: 1982 to 1985." *Armed Forces and Society* 13 (Winter 1987): 215–233.

Bennett, Douglas C., and Sharpe, Kenneth E. "The State as Banker and as Entrepreneur: The Last Resort Character of the Mexican State's Economic Intervention, 1917–1970." *Comparative Politics* 12 (January 1980): 165–185.

Bittencourt, Getúlio. *A Quinta Estrela: Como se Tenta Fazer um Presidente no Brasil*. São Paulo: Editora Ciências Humanas, 1978.

Black, Jan Knippers. "The Military and Political Decompression in Brazil." *Armed Forces and Society* 6 (Summer 1980): 625–638.

Borón, Atilio A. "De la Política a la Guerra. Notas Sobre los Orígenes de la Militarización de la Cultura Política en la Argentina." EURAL, Documento de Trabajo No. 14/86. Buenos Aires, 1986.

Bourdieu, Pierre. *Ce que parler veut dire*. Paris: Fayard, 1982.

Boyd, Carolyn P., and Boyden, James. "The Armed Forces and the Transition to Democracy in Spain." In *Politics and Change in Spain*, edited by T.D. Lancaster and G. Provost, pp. 94–124. New York: Praeger Publishers, 1985.

Brazil, Assembléia Nacional Constituinte, Comissão da Organização Eleitoral, Partidária e Garantias Das Instituições, Subcomissão de Defesa do Estado, da Sociedade e de sua Segurança. *Anteprojeto: Relatório*. Brasília, May 1987.

Brazil, Estado-Maior das Forças Armadas, Escola Superior de Guerra, Associação dos Diplomados da Escola Superior de Guerra. *Almanaque*. Rio de Janeiro, 1984.

Brazil, Estado-Maior das Forças Armadas, Escola Superior de Guerra. *Complementos da Doutrina*. Rio de Janeiro, 1981.

———. *Doutrina Básica*. Rio de Janeiro, 1979.

———. *Fundamentos da Doutrina*. Rio de Janeiro, 1981.

Brazil, Ministério do Exército, Departamento Geral do Pessoal, Diretoria de Cadastro e Avaliação. *Oficiais: Almanaque do Pessoal Militar do Exército*. Rio de Janeiro: EGGCF, 1974.

Brazil, Ministério do Exército, Centro de Comunicação Social do Exército. *Temas Constitucionais: Subsídios*. Brasília, 1987.

Breckinridge, Scott D. *The C.I.A. and the U.S. Intelligence System*. Boulder, Colorado: Westview Press, 1986.

Bresser Pereira, Luis Carlos. *O Colapso de uma Aliança de Classes*. São Paulo: Editora Brasiliense, 1978.

Brigagão, Clóvis. *O Mercado da Segurança: Ensaios sobre Economia Política da Defesa*. Rio de Janeiro: Editora Nova Fronteira, 1984.

Brown, Cynthia, ed. *With Friends Like These: The Americas Watch Report on Human Rights and U.S. Policy in Latin America*. New York: Pantheon Press, 1985.

Brzezinski, Zbigniew. *Power and Principle: Memoirs of the National Security Advisor, 1977–1981*. New York: Farrar, Straus and Giroux, 1983.

Camargo, Aspásia and Góes, Walder de. *Meio Século de Combate: Diálogo com Cordeiro de Farias*. Rio de Janeiro: Editora Nova Fronteira, 1981.

Campos Coelho, Edmundo. *Em Busca da Identidade: O Exército e a Política na Sociedade Brasileira*. Rio de Janeiro: Editora Forense-Universitária, 1976.

————. "A Instituição Militar No Brasil." *Boletim Informativo e Bibliográfico de Ciências Sociais* 19 (1985): 5–20.

Cardoso, Fernando Henrique. "O Papel dos Empresários no Processo de Transição: O Caso Brasileiro." *Dados* 26 (1983): 9–27.

————. "Associated-Dependent Development and Democratic Theory." In *Democratizing Brazil: Problems of Transition and Consolidation*, edited by Alfred Stepan. New York: Oxford University Press, forthcoming.

Chauí, Marilena. *Cultura e Democracia: O Discurso Competente e Outras Falas*. São Paulo: Editora Moderna, 1982.

Clark, Robert P. *The Basque Insurgents: ETA, 1952–1980*. Madison: The University of Wisconsin Press, 1984.

Collier, David., ed. *The New Authoritarianism in Latin America*. Princeton: Princeton University Press, 1979.

Comblin, Joseph. *A Ideologia da Segurança Nacional: O Poder Militar na América Latina*. Rio de Janeiro: Editora Civilização Brasileira, 1980.

Crassweller, Robert D. *Trujillo: The Life and Times of a Caribbean Dictator*. New York: The Macmillan Company, 1966.

Dahl, Robert A. *Who Governs? Democracy and Power in an American City*. New Haven: Yale University Press, 1961.

———. *Polyarchy: Participation and Opposition*. New Haven: Yale University Press, 1971.

———. *Controlling Nuclear Weapons; Democracy versus Guardianship*. Syracuse: Syracuse University Press, 1985.

Della Cava, Ralph. "The 'People's Church,' the Vatican and the Abertura." In *Democratizing Brazil: Problems of Transition and Consolidation*, edited by Alfred Stepan. New York: Oxford University Press, forthcoming.

Diniz, Eli and Boschi, Renato. *Empresariado Nacional e Estado no Brasil*. Rio de Janeiro: Editora Forense-Universitária, 1978.

Dreifuss, René Armand. *1964: A Conquista do Estado, Ação Política, Poder e Golpe de Classe*. Petrópolis: Vozes, 1981.

Dreifuss, René Armand, and Soares Dulci, Otávio. "As Forças Armadas e a Política." In *Sociedade e Política no Brasil Pós-1964*, edited by Bernardo Sorj and Maria Hermínia Tavares de Almeida, pp. 87–117. São Paulo: Editora Brasiliense, 1983.

Evans, Peter; Rueschemeyer, Dietrich; and Skocpol, Theda, eds. *Bringing the State Back In*. New York: Cambridge University Press, 1985.

Fain, Tyrus G., ed. *The Intelligence Community: History, Organization and Issues*. New York and London: R. R. Bowker Co., 1977.

Faligot, Roger, and Krop, Pascal. *La Piscine: Les services secrets français, 1944–1984*. Paris: Editions du Seuil, 1985.

Figueiredo, Eurico de Lima. *Os Militares e a Democracia: Análise Estrutural da Ideologia do Presidente Castelo Branco*. Rio de Janeiro: Graal, 1980.

Fishlow, Albert. "A Tale of Two Presidents: The Political Economy of Crisis Management." In *Democratizing Brazil: Problems of Transition and Consolidation*, edited by Alfred Stepan. New York: Oxford University Press, forthcoming.

Fitch, John Samuel. *The Military Coup d'Etat as a Political Process: Ecuador, 1948–1976*. Baltimore: The Johns Hopkins University Press, 1977.

Fitch, John Samuel. "Theoretical Model: Core Assumptions; Assessment of Civil-Military Tensions and Short-term Coup Risk." Working draft prepared for the Inter-American Dialogue, Washington, D.C., May 1987.

Flynn, Peter. *Brazil: A Political Analysis*. Boulder, Colorado: Westview Press, 1980.

Fontana, Andrés. *Fuerzas Armadas, Partidos Políticos y Transición a la Democracia en Argentina*. Buenos Aires: Estudios CEDES, 1984.

—————. "De la Crisis de Malvinas a la Subordinación Condicionada: Conflictos Intramilitares y Transición Política en Argentina." The Helen Kellogg Institute for International Studies, University of Notre Dame, Working Paper 74, August 1986.

—————. "Fuerzas Armadas y Consolidación Democrática en Argentina." Paper prepared for a conference on "Fuerzas armadas y democratización en América Latina," held at the University of Campinas, Brazil, November 18–19, 1986.

—————. "Political Decision Making by a Military Corporation: Argentina, 1976–1983." Ph.D. dissertation, The University of Texas at Austin, 1987.

Foucault, Michel. "Truth and Power," and "Power and Strategies." Both in *Power and Knowlege: Selected Interviews and Other Writings, 1972–1977*, edited by Colin Gordon, pp. 109–133 and 134–145. New York: Pantheon Books, 1980.

Garretón, Manuel Antonio. *El Proceso Político Chileno*. Santiago: FLACSO, 1983.

—————. *Dictaduras y Democratización*. Santiago: FLACSO, 1984.

Gaspari, Elio. *Geisel e Golbery: O Sacerdote e o Feiticeiro*. São Paulo: draft manuscript, 1986.

Giddens, Anthony. *A Contemporary Critique of Historical Materialism*. Berkeley: University of California Press, 1981.

Gillespie, Charles Guy. "Party Strategies and Redemocratization: Theoretical and Comparative Perspectives on the Uruguayan Case." Ph.D. dissertation, Yale University, 1987.

Góes, Walder de. *O Brasil do General Geisel: Estudo do Processo de Tomada de Decisão no Regime Militar-Burocrático*. Rio de Janeiro: Editora Nova Fronteira, 1978.

————. "O Novo Regime Militar no Brasil." *Dados* 27 (1984): 361–376.

Golbery, (General) do Couto e Silva. *Conjuntura Política Nacional: O Poder Executivo e Geopolítica do Brasil*. Rio de Janeiro: Livraria José Olýmpio Editora, 1981.

Gonzáles García, Manuel. "Las Fuerzas Armadas: Pariente Pobre del Régimen de Franco." In *España en Crisis: La Evolución y Decadencia del Régimen de Franco*, edited by Paul Preston, pp. 61–91. Madrid: Fondo de Cultura Económica, 1977.

Gramsci, Antonio. *Selections From the Prison Notebooks*, edited by Quintin Hoare and Geoffrey Nowell Smith. New York: International Publishers, 1971.

Hansen, Roy Allen. "Military Culture and Organizational Decline: A Study of the Chilean Army." Ph.D. dissertation, University of California at Los Angeles, 1968.

Herz, John H., ed. *From Dictatorship to Democracy: Coping with the Legacies of Authoritarianism and Totalitarianism*. Westport, Connecticut, and London: Greenwood Press, 1982.

Hilton, Stanley E. "The Brazilian Military: Changing Strategic Perceptions and the Question of Mission." *Armed Forces and Society* 13 (Spring 1987): 329–352.

Hoffmann, Helga. "Pobreza e Propriedade no Brasil: O Que Está Mudando?" In *A Transição Incompleta: Brasil Desde 1945*, edited by Edmar Bacha and Herbert S. Klein, vol. 2, pp. 61–101. Rio de Janeiro and São Paulo: Editora Paz e Terra, 1986.

Hopple, Gerald W., and Watson, Bruce W., eds. *The Military Intelligence Community*. Boulder, Colorado: Westview Press, 1985.

Huntington, Samuel P. *Political Order in Changing Societies*. New Haven: Yale University Press, 1968.

Keck, Margaret. "The 'New Unionism' in the Brazilian Transition." In *Democratizing Brazil: Problems of Transition and Consolidation*, edited by Alfred Stepan. New York: Oxford University Press, forthcoming.

Koutzii, Flávio, ed. *Nova República: Um Balanço.* São Paulo: L & PM Editores, 1986.

Kucinski, Bernardo. *Abertura, a História de uma Crise.* São Paulo: Editora Brasil Debates, 1982.

"La Cúpula Cívico-Militar," *Carta Política*, Buenos Aires, May 1976, 32–35.

Lagôa, Ana. *SNI: Como Nasceu, Como Funciona.* São Paulo: Editora Brasiliense, 1983.

Lamounier, Bolivar. " 'Authoritarian Brazil' Revisited: The Impact of Elections on the Abertura." In *Democratizing Brazil: Problems of Transition and Consolidation*, edited by Alfred Stepan. New York: Oxford University Press, forthcoming.

Landi, Oscar. *El Discurso Sobre lo Posible (La Democracia y el Realismo Político).* Buenos Aires: Estudios CEDES, 1984.

Lazarsfeld, Paul, and Rosenberg, Morris, eds. *The Language of Social Research: A Reader in the Methodology of Social Research.* Glencoe, Illinois: Free Press, 1955.

Lerin, François, and Torres, Cristina. *Les transformations institutionelles de L'Uruguay (1973–1977).* Paris: Problèmes d'Amerique Latine, 1978.

Linz, Juan J. "The Future of an Authoritarian Situation or the Institutionalization of an Authoritarian Regime: The Case of Brazil." In *Authoritarian Brazil: Origins, Policies, and Future*, edited by Alfred Stepan, pp. 233–254. New Haven and London: Yale University Press, 1973.

———. "Totalitarian and Authoritarian Regimes." In *Handbook of Political Science*, edited by Fred Greenstein and Nelson Polsby, vol. 3, pp. 175–411. Reading, Massachusetts: Addison-Wesley Publishing Company, 1975.

———. "The Transition from an Authoritarian Regime to Democracy in Spain: Some Thoughts for Brazilians." Paper delivered at the "Conference on Democratizing Brazil," Yale University, New Haven, March 2, 1983.

Linz, Juan J., and Stepan, Alfred. "Political Crafting of Democratic Consolidation or Destruction: European and South American Comparisons." Paper prepared for delivery at the conference on Reinforcing Democracy in the Americas, The

Carter Presidential Center, Atlanta, Georgia, November 17–18, 1986.

Lowenthal, Abraham F., and Fitch, J. Samuel, eds. *Armies and Politics in Latin America*. Rev. ed. New York: Holmes and Meier, 1986.

Lowenthal, Mark M. *U.S. Intelligence: Evolution and Anatomy*. New York: Praeger/Georgetown University Center for International and Strategic Studies, 1984.

Lukes, Stephen. *Power: A Radical View*. London: Macmillan, 1974.

Mainwaring, Scott. "Grass Roots Popular Movements and the Struggle for Democracy: Nova Iguaçu." In *Democratizing Brazil: Problems of Transition and Consolidation*, edited by Alfred Stepan. New York: Oxford University Press, forthcoming.

Marichy, Jean-Pierre. "The Central Organization of Defense in France." In *Central Organizations of Defense*, edited by Martin Edmonds, pp. 35–65. Boulder, Colorado: Westview Press, 1985.

Marx, Karl. *The 18th Brumaire of Louis Bonaparte*. New York: International Publishers, 1963.

Miguens, José Enrique. *Honor Militar, Conciencia Moral y Violencia Terrorista*. Buenos Aires: Sudamericana/Planeta, 1986.

Moneta, Carlos J. "Fuerzas Armadas y Gobierno Constitucional Después de Malvinas: Hacia Una Nueva Relación Cívico-Militar." In *La Reforma Militar*, edited by Carlos J. Moneta, Ernesto López, and Aníbal Romero, pp. 7–100. Buenos Aires: Editorial Legasa, 1984.

Munizaga, Giselle. *El Discurso Público de Pinochet: Un Análisis Semiológico*. Buenos Aires: CLACSO, 1983.

*Nunca Más: The Report of the Argentine National Commission of the Disappeared*. New York: Farrar, Straus, and Giroux, 1986.

O'Donnell, Guillermo. *Modernization and Bureaucratic-Authoritarianism: Studies in South American Politics*. Berkeley: Institute of International Studies, University of California, 1973.

O'Donnell, Guillermo; Schmitter, Philippe C.; and Whitehead, Laurence, eds. *Transitions From Authoritarian Rule: Prospects for Democracy.* Baltimore and London: The Johns Hopkins University Press, 1986.

Oseth, John M. *Regulating U.S. Intelligence Operations: A Study in Definition of the National Security Interest.* Lexington: The University of Kentucky Press, 1985.

Payne, Stanley G. "Modernization of the Armed Forces." In *The Politics of Democratic Spain*, edited by Stanley G. Payne, pp. 181–196. Chicago: The Chicago Council on Foreign Relations, 1986.

Perelli, Carina, "Amnistía sí, amnistía no, amnistía puede ser
. . . La constitución histórica de un tema político en el Uruguay de la postransición." Paper delivered at a conference on Civil-Military Relations and Democracy in Latin America, American University, Washington, D.C., January 7, 1987.

————. *Convencer o Someter: El Discurso Militar.* Montevideo: Ediciones de la Banda Oriental, 1987.

Philip, George. *The Military in South American Politics.* London: Croom Helm, 1985.

Pinheiro, Paulo Sérgio. "Polícia e Crise Política: O Caso das Polícias Militares." In *A Violência Brasileira*, edited by Roberto da Matta et al., pp. 57–97. São Paulo: Editora Brasiliense, 1982.

Poulantzas, Nicos. *Political Power and Social Classes.* London: New Left Books, 1973.

————. *State, Power and Socialism.* London: New Left Books, 1978.

Rabello Duarte, Celina. "Imprensa e Redemocratização no Brasil." *Dados* 26 (1983): 181–195.

*Revista Española de Investigaciones Sociológicas* 36 (October–December 1986). Special issue devoted to "El Papel de las Fuerzas Armadas en la Transición Española."

Rial, Juan. "Las Reglas del Juego Electoral en Uruguay y sus Implicaciones." CIESU, Serie Documentos de Trabajo, DT 88, Montevideo, 1985.

————. "Las Fuerzas Armadas: Soldados-Políticos Garantes de la Democracia?" CIESU, Serie Documentos de Trabajo, DT 132/86, Montevideo, 1986.

————. "Las Fuerzas Armadas en tanto Actor Político en los Procesos de Re(Construcción) de la Democracia en América Latina." Paper prepared for delivery at a conference on Civil-Military Relations and Democracy in Latin America, American University, Washington, D.C., January 7, 1987.

Richards, Paul G., and Lindle, Allan. "Toward a New Test Ban Regime." *Issues in Science and Technology* 3 (1987): 101–108.

Richelson, Jeffrey T. *The United States Intelligence Community*. Cambridge, Massachusetts: Ballinger, 1985.

————. *Sword and Shield: The Soviet Intelligence and Security Apparatus*. Cambridge, Massachusetts: Ballinger, 1986.

Rizzo de Oliveira, Eliezer. "Conflits militaires et décisions sous la présidence du Général Geisel (1974–1979)." In *Les partis militaires au Brésil*, edited by Alain Rouquié, pp. 105–140. Paris: Presses de la Fondation Nationale des Sciences Politiques, 1980.

————, ed. *Militares: Pensamento e Ação Política*. Campinas, São Paulo: Editora Papirus, 1987.

Rodrigo, Fernando. "El Papel de las Fuerzas Armadas Españolas Durante la Transición Política: Algunas Hipótesis Básicas." *Revista Internacional de Sociología* 43 (April–June 1985): 349–369.

————. "Las Fuerzas Armadas y la Transición. *Revista de Occidente*, no. 54 (November 1985): 57–67.

Ronning, Neale C., and Keith, Henry H. "Shrinking Political Arena: Military Government Since 1964." In *Perspectives on Armed Politics in Brazil*, edited by Henry H. Keith and Robert A. Hayes, pp. 225–252. Tempe, Arizona: Center for Latin American Studies, Arizona State University, 1976.

Rouquié, Alain. *O Estado Militar na América Latina*. São Paulo: Alfa-Omega, 1984.

————, ed. *Les partis militaires au Brésil*. Paris: Presses de la Fondation Nationale des Sciences Politiques, 1980.

Russett, Bruce, and Stepan, Alfred. "The Military in America: New Parameters, New Problems, New Approaches." In *Military Force and American Society*, edited by Bruce Russett and Alfred Stepan, pp. 3–16. New York: Harper and Row, 1973.

Selcher, Wayne A. *Brazil's Multilateral Relations: Between First and Third Worlds*. Boulder, Colorado: Westview Press, 1978.

Skidmore, Thomas. "Brazil's Slow Road to Democratization." In *Democratizing Brazil: Problems of Transition and Consolidation*, edited by Alfred Stepan. New York: Oxford University Press, forthcoming.

Stepan, Alfred. *The Military in Politics: Changing Patterns in Brazil*. Princeton: Princeton University Press, 1971.

―――. "The New Professionalism of Internal Warfare and Military Role Expansion." In *Authoritarian Brazil: Origins, Policies and Future*, edited by Alfred Stepan, pp. 47–68. New Haven: Yale University Press, 1973.

―――. *The State and Society: Peru in Comparative Perspective*. Princeton: Princeton University Press, 1978.

―――. "Political Leadership and Regime Breakdown: Brazil." In *The Breakdown of Democratic Regimes: Latin America*, edited by Juan J. Linz and Alfred Stepan, pp. 110 137. Baltimore and London: The Johns Hopkins University Press, 1978.

―――. "O Que Estão Pensando os Militares?" *Novos Estudos CEBRAP* 2 (July 1983): 2–7.

―――. "State Power and Civil Society in the Southern Cone of Latin America." In *Bringing the State Back In*, edited by Peter Evans, Dietrich Rueschemeyer, and Theda Skocpol, pp. 317–343. New York and Cambridge: Cambridge University Press, 1985.

―――. "Paths Towards Redemocratization: Theoretical and Comparative Considerations." In *Transitions from Authoritarian Rule: Comparative Perspectives*, edited by Guillermo O'Donnell, Philippe C. Schmitter, and Laurence Whitehead, pp. 64–84, 170–174. Baltimore and London: The Johns Hopkins University Press, 1986.

————, ed. *Democratizing Brazil: Problems of Transition and Consolidation.* New York: Oxford University Press, forthcoming.

Stockholm International Peace Research Institute. *World Armaments and Disarmament: SIPRI Yearbook, 1986.* New York: Taylor and Francis.

Stumpf, André Gustavo, and Pereira Filho, Merval. *A Segunda Guerra: Sucessão de Geisel.* São Paulo: Editora Brasiliense, 1979.

Sykes, Lynn R. and Evernden, Jack F. "The Verification of a Comprehensive Nuclear Test Ban." *Scientific American* 247 (October 1982): 47–55.

Trebat, Thomas J. *Brazil's State-Owned Enterprises: A Case Study of the State as Entrepreneur.* New York and Cambridge: Cambridge University Press, 1983.

United States, U.S. Arms Control and Disarmament Agency. *World Military Expenditures and Arms Transfers, 1985.* ACDA Publication 123.

United States, Congressional Research Service. Lowenthal, Mark M. "The National Security Council: Organizational History." Report 78–104f, Washington, D.C., June 27, 1978.

————. "The Central Intelligence Agency: Organizational History." Report 78–168f, Washington, D.C., August 4, 1978.

Uruguay, Junta de Comandantes en Jefe. *La Subversión.* Montevideo, 1976.

————. *El Proceso Político.* Montevideo, 1978.

Valenzuela, Arturo. *The Breakdown of Democratic Regimes: Chile.* Baltimore and London: The Johns Hopkins University Press, 1978.

Vanossi, Jorge Reinaldo. "Reflexiones sobre el Nuevo Régimen Institutional Argentino." *Carta Política.* Buenos Aires, June 1976, 41–50.

Varas, Augusto; Agüero, Felipe; and Bustamante, Fernando. *Chile, Democracia, Fuerzas Armadas.* Santiago: Flacso, 1980.

Vidal, Hernán. "The Politics of the Body: The Chilean Junta and the Anti-Fascist Struggle." *Social Text: Theory/Culture/Ideology* (Summer 1979): 104–119.

Weber, Max. "Politics as a Vocation," and "Science as a Vocation." Both in *From Max Weber: Essays in Sociology*, pp. 77–128 and 129–156, edited and trans. by H. H. Gerth and C. Wright Mills, New York and Oxford: Oxford University Press, 1946.

Weffort, Francisco. "Why Democracy?" In *Democratizing Brazil: Problems of Transition and Consolidation*, edited by Alfred Stepan. New York: Oxford University Press, forthcoming.

Williams, John Hoyt. "Brazil: Giant of the Southern Cone." *National Defense* (November 1982): 16–20.

————. "Brazil: A New Giant in the Arms Industry." *Atlantic Monthly* (August 1984): 24–27.

World Bank. *World Development Report, 1984* and *1985*.

# INDEX

**Library of Congress Cataloging-in-Publication Data**

Stepan, Alfred C.
  Rethinking military politics.

  Bibliography: p.     Includes index.
  1. Brazil—Politics and government—1964–1985. 2. Brazil—Politics and government—1985–   . 3. Southern Cone of South America—Politics and government. 4. Brazil—Armed Forces—Political activity—History—20th century. 5. Southern Cone of South America—Armed Forces—Political activity—History—20th century. 6. Civil-military relations—Brazil—History—20th century. 7. Civil-military relations—Southern Cone of South America—History—20th century. I. Title.
  F2538.25.S79 1987    322′.5′0981    87–4537
  ISBN 0–691–07750–9 (alk. paper)
  ISBN 0–691–02274–7 (pbk. : alk. paper)